An Instant Playscript

# House
# of the Sun

Sudha Bhuchar and
Kristine Landon-Smith

Adapted from the novel by

Meira Chand

London
NICK HERN BOOKS

TAMASHA PLAYS

## An Instant Playscript

*House of the Sun*, adapted from the novel by Meira Chand,
first published in Great Britain in 1999 as a paperback original
by Nick Hern Books Limited, 14 Larden Road, London W3 7ST

Published jointly by Nick Hern Books and Tamasha Theatre Company

Typeset by Country Setting, Kingsdown, Kent CT14 8ES
Printed and bound in Great Britain

ISBN 1 85459 447 8

A CIP catalogue record for this book is available from
the British Library

*Funded by an Arts for Everyone grant
from the National Lottery through
the Arts Council of England*

## Tamasha Theatre Company

*Artistic Directors:* Sudha Bhuchar, Kristine Landon-Smith
*General Manager:* Kathy Bourne

'A major national Asian theatre company producing new writing theatre that draws from Asian literature and contemporary Asian life in Britain and abroad.'                                                    *London Arts Board*

'A highly successful company of national importance, producing high quality Asian theatre, that is visual, powerful and thought provoking.'
*The Arts Council of England*

Kristine Landon-Smith and Sudha Bhuchar formed Tamasha in 1989 to adapt *Untouchable* a classic Indian novel by Mulk Raj Anand. After an extremely successful debut the company has gone from strength to strength. Tamasha aims to reflect through theatre the Asian experience – from British Asian life to authentic accounts of life in the Indian sub-continent, adapting works of literature and classics to commissioning new work from a range of contemporary writers.

Tamasha Theatre Company, 11 Ronalds Road, London N5 1XJ

*Tel.* 0171 609 2411   *Fax.* 0171 609 2722
*E-mail:* general@tamasha.demon.co.uk
*Website:* http//www.tamasha.demon.co.uk

*House of the Sun* was first performed at Theatre Royal, Stratford East, London on 12 April 1991, with the following cast:

| | |
|---|---|
| MRS MURJANI, SUNITA WATUMAL | Sudha Bhuchar |
| MRS HATHIRAMANI | Charubala Chokshi |
| BHAI SAHIB, MR BHAGWANDAS, MR WATUMAL, HOSHIAR SINGH | Kaleem Janjua |
| SHAM | Ravi Kapoor |
| MOHAN, GOPAL | Amardeep Kaushal |
| REKHA, BIMLA | Shaheen Khan |
| MRS WATUMAL, PUPHI | Surendra Kochar |
| LATA, MEENA | Shobu McAuley |
| PADMA, SUSHU | Archie Panjabi |
| MRS SAMTANI, MRS BHAGWANDAS, DAIYA | Sakuntala Ramanee |
| LAKSHMI, PINKY | Sunetra Sarker |
| MR HATHIRAMAN | Madhav Sharma |
| RAJU, HARI | Dinesh Shukla |
| RANI, SWEEPER | Nina Wadia |

Other parts played by members of the Company

*Director* Kristine Landon-Smith
*Designer* Sue Mayes
*Lighting Designer* Richard Moffatt
*Sound Designer* Mike Furness
*Composer* Sarwar Sabri

## Characters

DR AGARWAL, *abortionist*
MR BHAGWANDAS, *jeweller, third-floor resident*
MRS BHAGWANDAS, *his wife*
BHAI SAHIB, *second-floor resident*
GOPAL, *liftman*
MR HATHIRAMANI, *former journalist, fourth-floor resident*
MRS HATHIRAMANI, *his illiterate wife*
PINKY LALWANI, *friend of Rani Murjani*
SUSHU, *friend of Rani Murjani*
MURLI MURJANI, *rich industrialist, seventh-floor resident*
MRS MURJANI, *his wife*
RANI MURJANI, *their daughter*
KISHIN PUMNANI, *former headmaster, seventh-floor resident*
REKHA PUMNANI, *his wife*
MEENA, *their married daughter*
SHAM, *their son*
LAKSHMI, *eldest unmarried daughter*
PADMA, *younger, unmarried daughter*
PUPHI, *widowed sister of Kishin Pumnani*
RAJU, *Mr and Mrs Hathiramani's servant*
MRS SAMTANI, *mother in law to Lakshmi*
HARI SAMTANI, *husband of Lakshmi Pumnani*
MR WATUMAL, *factory owner, sixth-floor resident*
MRS WATUMAL, *his wife*
MOHAN WATUMAL, *their only son*
SUNITA WATUMAL, *unmarried daughter, aged 31*
LATA WATUMAL, *younger unmarried daughter, aged 29*
BIMLA, *Bhagwandas' servant*
HOSHIAR SINGH, *Murjani's servant*
DAIYA, *washerwoman, services all flats*
SWEEPER, *services all flats*

*The action of the play takes place in and around Sadhbela,*
*an apartment block in Bombay.*

## ACT ONE

### Scene One

*Early March (about the 12th). Climate: hot. Afternoon. Lights up on* MRS HATHIRAMANI *leaving her flat on the fourth floor. Moving downstairs she calls to* BHAI SAHIB *on the second floor.*

MRS HATHIRAMANI. Bhai Sahib! O Bhai Sahib!

*Lights up on* BHAI SAHIB*'s apartment – he is eating lunch in partitioned-off front room –* BHAI SAHIB*'s wife is also there.*

BHAI SAHIB. Oof, Mrs Hathiramani again! Can't a man eat in peace?

HIS WIFE. Only yesterday she was here.

BHAI SAHIB. Even if a cat walks in front of her she comes to me and says 'Bhai Sahib, this cat walked from left to right, tell me – what does it mean?' Next time if the cat walks from right to left again she comes thinking something bad is going to happen.

MRS HATHIRAMANI *has arrived at Bhai Sahib's flat, she comes inside and places an offering of cashew nut sweets under Guru Nanak's picture.*

MRS HATHIRAMANI. Han Om Bhai Sahib! O Bhai Sahib, anyone there? Do as you wish then – I know you are there. I am waiting. (*She sits and fans herself.*)

*We see and hear him finishing off his lunch in the other section of the room.*

BHAI SAHIB (*entering*). I was eating. Only daal and rice every day. Nowadays even for God people won't pay.

MRS HATHIRAMANI. I too can eat daal and rice every day and not complain.

BHAI SAHIB. But for people like you Mrs Hathiramani – you

have five different vegetables, saye bhaji, methi machi with dhodho chutney.

MRS HATHIRAMANI. And for you Bhai Sahib – imported video and television. So little room left for the temple.

BHAI SAHIB. Mrs Hathiramani, this I haven't purchased. It is a gift. In next block there is a rich man – his son was getting married – he wanted me to read his son and the wife to be's horoscope – with God's grace everything turned out right. In his happiness he gave it to me.

*She passes him her chart.*

BHAI SAHIB. Aatcha – what's the matter?

MRS HATHIRAMANI. Well you look at it and you tell me.

BHAI SAHIB. Here we are. Let us see what is happening in your Janam Kundli. Mangal is in the eleventh house exactly opposite to Shani Rahu. Budd Surya are together. Shani Rahu is entering the fifth house – the House of The Sun – das mein ghar ka malik panchmein ghar mein aa raha hè.

*His expression changes.*

MRS HATHIRAMANI. What is it Bhai Sahib? Is Mr Hathiramani going to be all right?

BHAI SAHIB. I did the prayers for Mr Hathiramani – he is all right, but Mrs Hathiramani for you – Saturn is coming into the House of The Sun.

MRS HATHIRAMANI. Aiee Allah!

BHAI SAHIB. Saturn is strong and will bring trouble. Lots of mental pressures can be expected. Fifth house is house of education and children.

MRS HATHIRAMANI. Bhai Sahib you know we have no children.

BHAI SAHIB. There will be influence on mental side. Expect a lot of tension on your brain.

MRS HATHIRAMANI. Please Bhai Sahib what can I do about it?

BHAI SAHIB. For three months Saturn will stay in your horoscope. It will not move out till June.

MRS HATHIRAMANI. But what can I do Bhai Sahib?

BHAI SAHIB. The only thing Saturn fears is a sapphire. Saturn will always stay away. It will be in your horoscope – but you wear a sapphire and no harm will come to you.

MRS HATHIRAMANI. Sapphire?

BHAI SAHIB. Han.

MRS HATHIRAMANI. I'll buy a sapphire. A cheap one will do?

BHAI SAHIB. Doesn't matter – expensive or cheap, result will be the same, but you must make sure it is the right sapphire for you.

MRS HATHIRAMANI. I'll go to P.B. Bhau.

BHAI SAHIB. Then you bring it back and I will perform some ritual to make it suitable.

MRS HATHIRAMANI. How much is it going to cost me?

BHAI SAHIB. Mrs Hathiramani your health is more important to me than money. And you know I am indebted to Mr Hathiramani for offering me this home when I came, without a single pai, from Sind.

MRS HATHIRAMANI. Already those prayers for Mr Hathiramani have cost me quite a lot.

BHAI SAHIB. Mrs Hathiramani, our astrology is the oldest science in the Vedas. I'm not a cowboy – you know I always give proper advice.

MRS HATHIRAMANI. Problem is Mr Hathiramani doesn't believe in these things – he's an educated man and educated men don't believe in horoscopes and now I have to ask him for money to pay, so how much is it going to cost me?

BHAI SAHIB. Just as you decide. Now let me take these sweets before the crows get to them. Jaysheree Krishna!

*She goes.* MRS HATHIRAMANI *crosses to the lift.*

MRS HATHIRAMANI. Mua Gopal! Lift! Mua! Humco marke phir aagye kya? You'll kill me before you come with your lift.

GOPAL *and* RAJU *come into focus on the ground floor sitting beside the lift.* MRS HATHIRAMANI *starts walking up the stairs to the third floor.*

## Scene Two

GOPAL. Today all day in the lift nothing happened. How will I earn my tea money?

RAJU. Get a better job as a cook.

GOPAL. You and your cooking. Think you'll be a chef at Taj Mahal Hotel?

RAJU. At least my Memsahib gives me home food three times a day.

GOPAL. Sala – this is not just a job. My father – he helped to build this Sadhbela. First there were two rooms only – one for Hathiramani Sahib and one for Bhagwandas Sahib. Then the others from Sind started coming – slowly more rooms were added, then more storeys and when the building was finished the co-operative made my father in charge of the lift. Now I'm the lift man. You know what that means?

RAJU. Han.

GOPAL. What? You need to know a lot of engineering.

RAJU. Kya?

GOPAL. Which button to press when. Which floor to stop on. It's a technical job. If I'm not there do they know how to use it?

RAJU. My job is also technical.

GOPAL. What technical? A little chilli here, bit of salt there and it's cooked.

MR MURJANI. Gopal! Lift!

GOPAL. There's that Murli Murjani – let him wait. Such a cheapskate! So rich but he never gives a tip. We should have a liftman's union – if something happens we strike.

RAJU. But it's such an easy job.

GOPAL. Lunchtime – Murli comes up, goes down. His driver comes down with Rani's tiffin then back up with empty tiffin and sala, your mother, she goes from 4th to 2nd, 2nd to 3rd, then back up to 4th.

RAJU. My memsahib needs the lift.

GOPAL. What does she do for you? Beats you and calls you donkey.

RAJU. She gave me two new shirts and two shorts at Holi.

GOPAL. When it suits her she treats you like her ladla chokra. She's still hoping by being kind to you even at her age she'll be rewarded with children.

RAJU. You should look after her – she's too old to walk up and down. You get paid for taking her.

GOPAL. How much? A hundred and fifty rupees. From there I have to buy tea, this, that and Mr Hathiramani's collecting for my pension. What do I want with a pension?

RAJU. For your wife and kids.

GOPAL. Who's going to marry me?

RAJU. That's true. No one will.

GOPAL. Who's going to marry you?

RAJU. I'm getting married.

GOPAL. Who to? Your mother going to find you someone?

RAJU. Rani. I've seen her from the back – jhun, jhun, jhun.

GOPAL. Sala.

MR MURJANI. Gopal! Lift!

GOPAL. OK Sahib – coming.

*GOPAL goes up in the lift to fetch MURLI MURJANI. On his way up he passes MRS HATHIRAMANI standing outside the Bhagwandas' flat which is a sea-facing flat on the third floor.*

MRS HATHIRAMANI. Laphunga! The co-operative doesn't pay you to gossip downstairs – you're wasting everyone's money. You know Mr Hathiramani is the secretary – it'll be brought up at the next meeting, you wait and see.

*GOPAL has by this time collected MURLI MURJANI from the seventh floor and is bringing him down – they pass MRS HATHIRAMANI and MURLI greets her coldly. MRS HATHIRAMANI knocks on the Bhagwandas' door.*

## Scene Three

MRS HATHIRAMANI. Oh that Murli Murjani!

MRS BHAGWANDAS. What is it Putali Bhen?

MRS HATHIRAMANI. Just gone down in the lift and he didn't greet me properly.

MRS BHAGWANDAS. He's a busy man. He must be going back to office. Mehrbani karé acchievio.

MRS HATHIRAMANI. When we fled Sind, he was still a child. On a refugee train from Karachi after Partition, he sat on Mr Hathiramani's lap and wet himself as he slept. Mr Hathiramani had only the trousers he wore when we were chased out by the Muslims. Not till we reached Delhi did Mr Hathiramani get more trousers at a refugee camp. Two months he carried on him the stain of Murli's pee. And just see he is such a big man – he can't speak to us now. See how money changes people.

MRS BHAGWANDAS. But in Sind also the Murjanis had money. They were great zamindars. Do you know they had the only Cadillac in Sind? They had to leave it there.

MRS HATHIRAMANI. I'm talking about money Murli has made in Bombay. This money is new money, the other was old. Both have a different effect.

MRS BHAGWANDAS. For so many years in Sind we were happy. We Sindhi Hindus and Muslims were very friendly. We got along famously. Who would have thought that this could happen. Tain chai pianda?

MRS HATHIRAMANI. Not tea Jashoti. It's too hot for tea.

MRS BHAGWANDAS. Nimbu paani?

MRS HATHIRAMANI. Han but I won't stay long. I've come to see P.B. Bhau.

MRS BHAGWANDAS. He's having a nap just now – should wake up soon. Bimla!

BIMLA. Han Memsahib.

MRS BHAGWANDAS. Do Nimbu Paani and bring the mithai that Mrs Murjani sent.

BIMLA. Which glass shall I bring?

MRS BHAGWANDAS. Any.

BIMLA *goes.*

MRS BHAGWANDAS. Poor woman! If it wasn't for Mr
Bhagwandas' kindness she would have been left behind in
Sind.

MRS HATHIRAMANI. Han at the mercy of those Muslims.

VEGETABLE SELLER *calls from offstage.*

MRS BHAGWANDAS. Forty years she's been with us – we
tried to get her married – but what can you do? Only four
bangles her widowed mother left us and still we are looking
after her.

VEGETABLE SELLER, *now onstage, calls.*

MRS HATHIRAMANI. Oh yes P.B. Bhau helped so many
people. Took their jewellery – gave them money. Remember
our two bedroom apartment was an open house for refugees?

MRS BHAGWANDAS. At night you couldn't get to the
bathroom for all the bodies sleeping on the floor.

MRS HATHIRAMANI. Well we all had to help each other,
we're not the sort to go begging for charity.

MRS BHAGWANDAS. All those papads and achaars we made
to raise the money for this building.

MRS HATHIRAMANI. Now everyone is resettled thanks to
P.B. Bhau and Mr Hathiramani.

MRS BHAGWANDAS. Yes but now it's interpreted wrongly –
people when they see we have secured this sea-facing flat
they think we tried to make money from the Partition. No –
it was a charitable gesture – it cost Mr Bhagwandas money –
after all who's going to buy second-hand mangal sutra? He
had to melt everything down – separate the beads from the
gold – it cost him more money than it was worth.

BIMLA *comes with the drinks and the sweets.*

MRS HATHIRAMANI. Oh no ice?

MRS BHAGWANDAS. You want ice? It's quite cold.

BIMLA. Straight from fridge Memsahib.

MRS HATHIRAMANI. OK Teek aie.

MRS BHAGWANDAS. No. No, if you want ice – there is ice.

MRS HATHIRAMANI. Bus teek aiena.

MRS BHAGWANDAS. Bimla – go and get ice for Mrs Hathiramani.

BIMLA. Memsahib electricity went off – there's no ice.

MRS BHAGWANDAS. When did electricity go off – last night? Why didn't you put ice in this morning? OK you go down now and buy some. (*She goes.*) Namourad! Doesn't do anything properly. Forty years and still she hasn't learnt.

MRS HATHIRAMANI. Well it is not in the Sindhi nature to be a servant.

MRS BHAGWANDAS. Yes – should have got a Maharashtran or a boy from U.P. Could have trained them properly. But we can't throw her out can we?

MRS HATHIRAMANI. Well also it's so difficult to find servants in Bombay nowadays.

MRS BHAGWANDAS. Han. Thoro khaona. (*Offering sweets.*)

MRS HATHIRAMANI. Oh half kilo box! To me Mrs Murjani sent only quarter. Does she think we never meet? – I won't find out?

MRS BHAGWANDAS. No no, I'm sure she was just thinking of Mr Hathiramani's diabetes.

MRS HATHIRAMANI (*taking a sweet*). They are for Mrs Murjani's nephew's wedding you know. The girl is from Gibraltar. Where is this Gibraltar?

MRS BHAGWANDAS. All our Sindhis settled in Foreign bring their girls here to get married.

MRS HATHIRAMANI. These are not good marriages. The girls from Foreign have loose morals. Mrs Murjani knows she could have come to us – we would have found someone suitable – she's too proud.

MR BHAGWANDAS *enters.*

MR BHAGWANDAS. Ram Ram Mrs Hathiramani. Kiya aaiyo.

14

MRS HATHIRAMANI. Han Om P.B. Bhau.

MR BHAGWANDAS. Han Om. How are you?

MRS HATHIRAMANI. Truth is bhau – things are not so good. Horoscope is very bad. Saturn is in The House of The Sun.

MR BHAGWANDAS. Oh Saturn, Shani is very bad.

MRS HATHIRAMANI. Bhai Sahib says I should buy a sapphire.

MR BHAGWANDAS. Bhai Sahib is indeed correct. You have a problem with Saturn – you leave the rest to me.

MRS HATHIRAMANI. Any cheap quality will do.

MR BHAGWANDAS. Mrs Hathiramani I have been a jeweller since pre Partition in Sukkur, Sind. You don't worry – I will find for you the best.

MRS HATHIRAMANI. Ah yes even in Rohri across the river we knew of your family's reputation.

MR BHAGWANDAS. But people from Rohri didn't trust us. They were suspicious of our wealth.

MRS HATHIRAMANI. That was Sind. But now in this Bombay where we would we be without each other?

MR BHAGWANDAS. Yes – here we must all stick together. In my business I employ only Sindhis – if something goes wrong you know which door to knock on. If I employ a Gujerati, Maharashtran, Madrasi – half the time they're going to be fighting over Bombay – not working for me.

MRS BHAGWANDAS. We are not interested in politics.

MR BHAGWANDAS. Here – this will be the correct one for the job.

MRS HATHIRAMANI. Please set it in a ring – it must be touching my skin at all times.

MR BHAGWANDAS. No problem. It will be done straight away.

MRS HATHIRAMANI. Chango ma vanyati. Han Om. Aatcha Jashoti.

*She exits.*

## Scene Four

*The* MURJANI*'s penthouse apartment on the seventh floor.*
*We cross to this scene as* MRS HATHIRAMANI *is making her*
*journey back to her flat.* PINKY LALWANI, RANI MURJANI
*and* SUSHU *are talking.*

RANI. I just wish I lived somewhere else.

PINKY. Where do you want to live?

RANI. I want to live in England.

PINKY. You've never been there.

RANI. No, I've seen the men though.

*Laughs.*

PINKY. The trouble with you is, Rani – you don't assert
yourself – I mean you could actually be standing up for
yourself here. Instead you sit there and have these pipe
dreams about going abroad.

RANI. Its easy for you – your parents are really liberal. It's not
the same for me – I really wish I could be like you! You get
to do what you want.

PINKY. You can.

RANI. I can't baba.

SUSHU. Of course you can. You're lucky to be Amil. With my
backward Shikarpuri upbringing, I've had to fight for
everything I've got.

PINKY. Yaar – Sushu's right – Considering your mother's an
M.A. – nothing's rubbed off on you.

RANI. My mother's a hypocrite. That's something you have to
understand – she studied right – she's got an M.A. – you
know that – but then she also fought for me to get into
college – so now I'm in college and now I want to study –
she won't let me.

PINKY. Let's face it – most of our parents are hypocrites and
I mean, what is it? They study – then they get married and
they're dripping in their diamonds and saris.

16

RANI. What do you want me to do then? You want me to run away from home?

PINKY. You want to be sitting there like your mother having your rummy parties and dripping in your diamonds!

RANI. Of course not.

SUSHU. Pass me the cigs please. Pass me a cig, yaar. Thank-you.

RANI. Stop smoking Yaar Sushu.

SUSHU. Why?

RANI. It's not good for your health.

SUSHU. Good for the image though.

RANI. I suppose – give me one. (*Laughs.*)

PINKY. What do you think of Kamal? He's quite cute isn't he?

RANI. He is – yes he's lovely.

PINKY. You know something – believe it or not he's here to get married. Can you believe it?

RANI. Oooh! Who's he getting married to?

SUSHU. No.

PINKY. You know my aunt – she's come here with this silly idea – this guy who's grown up in America all his life and she thinks she can fix him up with some desi village girl. So he's doing the rounds.

RANI. Oh!

SUSHU. Do you like him then?

RANI. Actually he's all right.

PINKY. Oh what's this! What's this?

RANI. Don't start spreading rumours to my mother please.

PINKY. Aré – have us over for tea. I'll bring Kamal.

RANI. You'll have to dress him up like a girl before my mother lets him in.

PINKY. It'll be quite legitimate. I'll be there.

RANI. I suppose yaar. So Pinky, how's Girish?

PINKY. I'll chaperone you. Girish is fine.

RANI. Really, what's he doing now?

PINKY. He's at college – we're OK.

RANI. Is he going to England with you? You all getting married?

PINKY. Look I'm in no imminent danger – I'm going to Oxford and he's going to be here – so I'm not taking it too seriously.

VEGETABLE SELLER *enters, calling, crosses, then exits.*

SUSHU. I'm so bored. Life's so boring isn't it?

RANI. Um! So hot out here.

SUSHU. Stop cribbing. Put on the A.C.

PINKY. Rani – is there any more Limca?

RANI. Hoshiar Singh!

SUSHU. I'm sick of drinking these Limcas.

HOSHIAR SINGH. Memsahib.

RANI. OK so what do you want? Limca? Sushu?

PINKY. Han.

SUSHU. Gin and tonic.

RANI. Don't be funny. Teen Limca aur air conditioning lagado.

PINKY. Guess who I saw at 1900's? Rahoul Roy.

SUSHU. Oh I hate going there – it's full of socialites.

RANI. He was damn good in 'Aashki'.

PINKY. Are you joking? – he was so bloody awful they had to dub his voice.

RANI. Well you've got to admit he's quite cute. Don't you think so Sushu?

SUSHU. He's got a nice arse.

PINKY. Oh God I'm in such boringly juvenile company!

18

RANI. Oh – we forgot – your hero's Tom Cruise.

PINKY. Yeh sure – the Americans are so much nicer. – Our Indian men – they get married – then they get oily and paunchy.

RANI. So why are you dating an Indian then?

PINKY. Girish is different.

RANI. Well I hate Sindhi men – that's for sure. They're quite vile – all they want to do is booze and cultivate the right contacts.

PINKY. Well you better get used to them because you're going to be marrying one.

RANI. Don't be funny. I'm never marrying a Sindhi. I'm sick of being an Ani – Murjani, Lalwani I'm most definitely not going to be an Ani.

PINKY. Sushu's going to marry a Sindhi. Same caste and all.

SUSHU. I don't want to talk about marriage. I've still got my B.Comm to think of.

PINKY. Forget the B. Comm. You'll be packed off at eighteen to some stingy Shikarpuri.

SUSHU. I'm holding out till twenty-two.

PINKY. Eighteen, you'll see.

SUSHU. There'll be a Mahabharata.

RANI. What's the use of studying B.Comm if you're never going to use it?

SUSHU. Well if my husband's open minded – if he allowed me – I'd work.

RANI. Well I definitely want a career – I've got to do something.

PINKY. Why don't you do social work?

RANI. I'd love to but Mom won't hear of it – she says you have to go to such awful places to do it.

PINKY. So why does she sit on all those committees to help the underprivileged?

19

RANI. Oh she likes to think she's doing her share but all she does is put on her best sari and drink orange juice at some charity ball.

PINKY. You know you're going to end up like your sister in law.

RANI. Hey watch it!

PINKY. Asha was full of all this career talk – now look at her – all spreading and about to spawn.

RANI. I'm going to be auntie again.

SUSHU. Where are the drinks yaar? Hoshair Singh!

RANI. So won't you miss Girish when you go to Oxford?

PINKY. I've told you – we're just having a bit of fun. He's quite like me – very forward thinking.

SUSHU. Are you sleeping with him?

PINKY. None of your business.

RANI. Of course she is! She comes in with a big grin every day.

SUSHU. I hope you're taking precautions.

PINKY. What, do you think I'm going to Oxford all ready to spawn?

SUSHU. Accidents can happen.

PINKY. It might happen to people like you – Not to me!


**Scene Five**

MRS HATHIRAMANI *goes to her flat and rings the doorbell.*
RAJU *finally opens the door.*

MRS HATHIRAMANI. Raju! É Raju! Raju! Mua! Donkey! What were you doing?

RAJU. Memsahib I was sleeping.

MRS HATHIRAMANI. Sleeping! Is it the time to sleep?

RAJU. You know every afternoon I'm sleeping.

MRS HATHIRAMANI. Tea – get me tea. And where is your Sahib?

RAJU. Sleeping Memsahib.

MRS HATHIRAMANI. Sleeping. Nobody works in this house. Everyone has to sleep.

RAJU. You want tea?

MRS HATHIRAMANI. Don't answer back. Do you understand – don't ever answer back. I look after you so well. Who gave you these clothes? Who feeds you? Good food. Not these rubbish things that other servants get. That Gopal fellow is spoiling you.

RAJU. He's my friend.

MRS HATHIRAMANI. Why do you go there all the time? – down with him – that fellow never answers the lift – he never brought the lift up for me once today.

RAJU. He was sleeping.

MRS HATHIRAMANI. That's what I mean – everybody is sleeping – the whole building sleeps. Nothing else happens in Sadhbela. Go go and get me my tea.

*She goes into the bedroom and lies at* MR HATHIRAMANI's *feet.* MR HATHIRAMANI *is also dozing.*

MRS HATHIRAMANI. This is the weather – things go wrong. I have to do everything.

GOPAL *enters.*

GOPAL. Sahib.

MR HATHIRAMANI. Han. Han, come in.

MRS HATHIRAMANI. Mua! Smoking beedi in the house.

MR HATHIRAMANI. Let him. What's it to you?

MRS HATHIRAMANI. You're spoiling him.

RAJU *comes with the tea.*

MRS HATHIRAMANI. Who asked you to bring the tea? I want to sleep. (*She drops off to sleep.*)

MR HATHIRAMANI (*to* GOPAL, *indicating an article in a magazine*). Look what's happening in Grant Road – 'street prostitution'.

GOPAL. Kya Sahib?

MR HATHIRAMANI. When I started Hathiramani Electricals back in '47 there was none of this illicit trade. My shop is right there – what will it do to my business – God knows!

GOPAL. Sahib – three people working for you. You can stay home and write your diaries. Business will look after itself.

MR HATHIRAMANI. Very bad development in Bombay. It must be recorded in 'Miscellaneous Present'. The children in Sadhbela know only this Bombay – resettlement has eroded the Sindhi identity. There was a time when these flats were only for Sindhis – your father must have told you. Now with the prices going up they sell to the highest bidder.

GOPAL. Sahib Mr Murjani came early today for lunch.

MR HATHIRAMANI. What time?

GOPAL. About twelve. Twelve thirty.

MR HATHIRAMANI. Nahin, nahin. Don't twelve, twelve thirty me – I pay you to keep the exact details.

GOPAL. Sahib, I don't have a watch.

MR HATHIRAMANI. What happened to the one I gave you at the last Diwali?

GOPAL. My sister got married so I gave her husband a present.

MR HATHIRAMANI. Don't look at me like that. I'm not giving you another watch.

GOPAL. Nahin Sahib. You said keep proper time.

MR HATHIRAMANI. OK – exactly – what time?

GOPAL. Sadé bara – quarter to one.

MR HATHIRAMANI. Don't think you'll get another watch by telling me all this badé sara baje. Can't you read the clock tower?

GOPAL. I am in the lift. How will I see the clock tower?

MR HATHIRAMANI. Exact time.

GOPAL. Twelve twenty.

MR HATHIRAMANI. Ah – you have to pin them down.
(*Writing in diary.*) 'Arrivals – Murjani – twelve twenty pm.
Comments – early for lunch'.

GOPAL. If you're satisfied with that Sahib.

MR HATHIRAMANI. What do you mean satisfied? Don't I pay
you money?

GOPAL. Of course Sahib. Without you what would I do? Chai,
paani, beedi.

MR HATHIRAMANI. You should stop smoking.

GOPAL. Han Sahib.

MR HATHIRAMANI. Very bad. One of these days in the lift
you know all this oil you have – one day you're going to stub
your cigarette out in the lift – what is going to happen?

GOPAL. Sahib I won't smoke in the lift.

MR HATHIRAMANI. What will happen? It will catch fire – we
will all die.

GOPAL. Sahib with the insurance you'll be all right.

MR HATHIRAMANI. What insurance?

GOPAL. The co-operative society's.

MR HATHIRAMANI. What do you know about insurance?

GOPAL. Sahib – today driver also didn't come down with
Rani's tiffin so Murjani's were all home for lunch.

MR HATHIRAMANI. This morning we also received a quarter
kilo of sweets from them. Probably engagement of nephew
has been finalised. Have you talked to their servant?

GOPAL. Han Sahib – Hoshiar Singh wants too much money.

MR HATHIRAMANI. Too much money?

GOPAL. I said times are difficult. Hathiramani Sahib is not full
of money but he said I would need more before I got any
information.

MR HATHIRAMANI. You tell him Hathiramani Sahib doesn't succumb to bribery.

GOPAL. Sahib – month has ended and new month has begun.

MR HATHIRAMANI. OK what do I owe you?

GOPAL. Usual – tea money, beedi, paan.

MR HATHIRAMANI. OK – 75 rupees minus 15 for pension equals 60 rupees. One thing more, whenever my wife calls the lift . . .

GOPAL. I keep an eye on her Sahib. She went to Bhai Sahibs – then up to Bhagwandas Sahib and Bimla is telling me she has bought a sapphire for evil of Saturn.

MR HATHIRAMANI. Sapphire? Why don't you take her up and down? She has to do all this climbing.

GOPAL. Lift not working.

MR HATHIRAMANI. Your lift is never working. Come on now – any other information?

GOPAL. Sham Pumnani is back from Japan. He only uses the stairs – too ashamed to come in the lift.

MR HATHIRAMANI. Keep an eye on him. A man of few scruples must be watched.

GOPAL. Aatcha Sahib. Mehrbani Sahib.

MR HATHIRAMANI. 'Arrivals – Sham Pumnani from Japan. Comments – reputation unreliable'.


**Scene Six**

*The* PUMNANI *household. This could be the first time lapse – a couple of days bringing it to the 15th March. This is a seventh-floor flat – not sea facing.* LAKSHMI *is massaging* PUPHI's *feet.* MEENA *is there.* REKHA *comes out from behind the screen in the flat which partitions off where* KISHIN *is sleeping.*

REKHA. Your father's resting now – don't make too much noise. (*She comes back to the table where she is making chutney*) Padma – go and get the papads from the balcony, they must be dry by now. And don't forget the mango rind that Mrs Bhagwandas sent.

PADMA *does so.* SHAM *enters.*

REKHA. Sham beta – you ready for lunch?

SHAM. Han.

MEENA. Come back for food?

REKHA. Some toor daal, some selmaani and I've still a little ghee left for your paratha. Go and see your papa before you eat. (*He does so.*) Padma – bring the food for your brother.

PADMA. Mummy, I'm in a hurry – I've just got to eat and get back.

REKHA. OK, so bring the food – it's ready.

MEENA. How long can you keep this up? Papa's not stupid.

REKHA. Now is not the time. Better for him to think Sham is here on holiday.

PADMA. Meena didi will you leave that magazine for me when you go.

MEENA. Yeah – why not?

SHAM *comes back and sits down to his food.*

MEENA. Give him the chutney – how can he eat without chutney?

MEENA *goes and gets the chutney and bangs it on the table.*

REKHA. Meena – even if you do something nice – you have to spoil it – why couldn't you put it there nicely for him. Here Sham – Mrs Hathiramani sent it for us.

MEENA. Living on charity now, thanks to you.

REKHA. Eat son – you must keep up your strength.

MEENA. What for? Bumming around Bombay?

SHAM. Oh shut up Meena. You know I'm out looking for a job everyday.

REKHA. Leave it Meena. Your brother's only been back one week. He'll soon find a job – he's a B.A.

SHAM. Oh Mama! What use is a B.A. in Bombay? What was I doing before I went to Japan? Sitting on some street corner typing letters for the illiterate.

MEENA. At least you weren't thieving.

SHAM. Look Meena – you want to say something – let's have it out – now.

MEENA. One thing I asked for – one little electrical appliance, that's all I asked for and he couldn't even send that. Are you trying to tell me working in Japan for three years you couldn't do that?

REKHA. Meena.

SHAM. How many times must I tell you? I was just a junior in the business and my salary was low.

MEENA. So you started to steal. Where did that money go?

LAKSHMI. Bhaiya sent money for Papa's medicines.

MEENA. OK Lakshmi, so he sent a few medicines but Papa's still paralysed. Look at Mama – tired out from working day and night to look after him.

SHAM. Do you think I deliberately wanted to steal? How do you think I felt when everyone was writing to me asking for foreign this, foreign that and on top of that the medicines?

PADMA. Oh stop arguing everyone.

MEENA. You didn't send me anything – how can I keep my head up with my in laws?

REKHA. Your father is so ill and all you're worried about is your irons and your toasters. What your brother did, he did for the family.

MEENA. Why are you turning this round to make out it's my fault? You always do that. See that Puphi, she always sides with him.

PUPHI. Don't talk to me about him. I don't want to know.

REKHA. Don't be so hard on him. If his brothers hadn't died so young then the burden of looking after everybody wouldn't be on his shoulders alone. But that's Kismet.

SHAM. Mama – if you and Papa hadn't resigned yourself to fate you might have started again here.

REKHA. But son, your father always planned to go back to Sind.

SHAM. Papa's too sentimental – his heart was always tied up in his Sind model school. What use is our Amil education now in Bombay?

REKHA. Son we are Amils – you should be proud to come from an educated class.

SHAM. That's the past. The Amils might have prospered in Sind but here it's only money that matters. Look at us – we're living on charity – Papa always said a Sindhi would rather die than accept alms.

REKHA. Your father was a proud man – he was a headmaster – he taught half the people in this building. We had the keys to go and reopen the school – he couldn't do anything else. The day he realised we weren't going back to Sind he gave up on life.

SHAM. Papa could have adapted.

LAKSHMI. Please Bhiaya, Papa will hear.

SHAM. Many Amils started Bhaibund businesses and now look at them. Mr Murjani has a penthouse just across the corridor from us.

REKHA. Don't compare yourself to the Murjanis – in their blood there is business – in ours there is education.

SHAM. That's why I had to go crawling to Mr Murjani to arrange the job in Japan – my education couldn't pay the bills.

PUPHI. So you earned suspect Bhaibund money in Foreign to pay the bills and stole on top of that.

REKHA. Puphi Chupakar. Shanti kar bus. Ghano thio! His papa's just here.

27

MEENA. Papa knows. The whole of Bombay knows – I can't even walk down the street without people staring at me. My children come home from school saying Uncle Sham's a thief.

REKHA. You know Meena – I can't believe it – your papa and I brought you up to have a mind – you don't have to listen to that sort of thing. You know what Papa and I went through – we had to elope to get married. Do you think people weren't always staring at us?

MEENA. That was different.

REKHA. It wasn't any different.

MEENA. If you had any shame – you wouldn't be sitting here – you wouldn't show your face in this house until you had a job.

SHAM. Ma I'm going out.

REKHA. Come home for dinner beta.

### Scene Seven

SHAM *leaves the* PUMNANIs. *He bumps into* RANI *on the stairs.*

RANI. Hi. I heard you were back.

SHAM. I arrived a week ago.

RANI. So you recognise me or what?

SHAM. I miss the ankle socks – you haven't changed.

RANI. I take that as a compliment.

SHAM. It is.

RANI. How's your sister?

SHAM. Which one?

RANI. Lakshmi – I miss seeing her – I used to see her every day – now I'm at college – it's not possible.

SHAM. You're lucky to be at college.

RANI. What's Japan like?

SHAM. OK.

RANI. Are the people really as small as they say? (*They laugh.*)

RANI. I'm going to Japan one day.

RANI. Aatcha – I'll see you later then.

*During this scene as* RANI *and* SHAM *are coming down the stairs* DAIYA, *the dishwasher is walking upstairs to* WATUMAL*'s on sixth floor. As this scene ends she rings the* WATUMAL*'s bell.*

## Scene Eight

LATA *answers the door.*

LATA. Late again Daiya.

DAIYA. You know Lata Sahiba, I had to leave my daughter at Churchgate – buses are always full so it takes long time to come.

LATA. Aatcha. Koi baat nahin – the kitchen is out of order again – take the bartan out on the balcony.

DAIYA *goes to the balcony and starts dishes.*

DAIYA. Even at Murjani's lunch parties they're not so many dishes.

LATA. Daiya tum kam karo.

MRS WATUMAL (*entering*). Aiee. It is so hot outside. The taxi journey was terrible and then oonaje matha we had to meet some Parsi woman who looked down on my children because none of them are married.

MR WATUMAL. Well who told you to go to that Burmawalla all the way in Sion. Horoscopes are not going to help these children! They're too fussy.

MRS WATUMAL. It's all to do with evil eye. Mukhetha nazaar lagi vie. My medium Burmawalla told me. People are jealous because we came ahead of everyone from Sind with the money, not like them as refugees. So somebody has put nazaar – evil eye on us. She did give me the name – I don't want to say too loudly – Hathiramani – it was him that broke off Mohan's engagement.

SUNITA. Well the girl we were looking at for Mohan is distantly related to Mr Hathiramani.

MRS WATUMAL. So Mr Hathiramani must have said something about Mohan – even in Sind he had a reputation for twisting words.

LATA. He must have got out his crusty old diary and said Mohan's been sighted here there and everywhere.

SUNITA. He's not exactly a great catch – look at him – he's a total bum – he just bums around.

MOHAN. Papa I want to have a man to man chat with you.

MRS WATUMAL. Mr Hathiramani has always blamed you. He bought our land in Sukkur very cheaply – he thought Partition would never come – he wouldn't listen to your warnings. It's not our fault he had to leave it to the Muslims – now he bears a grudge.

MOHAN. Papa I need to discuss my plans with you.

MR WATUMAL. Mr Hathiramani is a gentleman. I'll talk to him face to face and see if it was him who advised against the engagement.

MRS WATUMAL. Don't you go near those Hathiramanis. You'll get deeper and deeper into their magic. Originally his family is from Hyderbad, Sind – why did he leave there to trouble us here and in Rohri and Sukkur?

MOHAN. Papa there's no point having the factory – you've got the union wallahs sitting on your head.

MR WATUMAL. What do you know? You've never done a day's work.

MOHAN. What is work? I'm working up here.

SUNITA. You're just a bloody wastrel.

MOHAN. That is where work is. It will bring fortunes that we've lost.

SUNITA. We wouldn't be sitting here rotting if we had a decent brother.

MOHAN. You want me to slog all my life for three thousand, five thousand bucks a month? – you must be joking. You've got to get the right opportunity. Once you've got that opportunity you've got to grab it!

LATA. You've got the opportunity – you've got the factory.

MRS WATUMAL. He's trying – he's my son – do you think he's not doing everything, but people are against him.

MOHAN. What's the point of the factory. Best idea – liquidate it – I'll invest the money properly.

DAIYA. Sunita – you take one dish, eat something, put it there. You take another dish, eat something, put it there. You think I have all day to do your bartan? Why don't you just take one plate like everybody else.

SUNITA. You just do that. I'm reducing – my new diet says I have to eat constantly and at regular intervals.

MR WATUMAL. It's my fault. I didn't train him. Right from the early age. We had a very good business but as blight hits a fine crop so our factory deteriorated.

LATA. Papa you spoilt him.

SUNITA. Everyday he goes to Papa – 100 bucks for coffee . . .

LATA. Yaar, promptly goes to the Taj and drinks it all.

MOHAN. I'm consulting people with business propositions.

LATA. Why don't you consult Papa? Papa's a good industrialist.

MOHAN. What is the point of spending 10 and getting 15 – when you can invest 10 and with growth it becomes 2,000 . . . ?

MRS WATUMAL. All bad luck – brought on us by people who are jealous. Mr Watumal went from selling china door to door in Sind to owning pen nib factory in Bombay, but still people don't give him the proper respect.

MR WATUMAL. My name was all over Bombay. If you looked at these adverts on the bridges 'If you want nibs, Watumal's the person'. You buy a pen – what do you see? 'Nib from Watumal.'

SUNITA. All his friends are loafers like him. Other girls have brothers – they introduce them to such catches. Look at Lata and me.

LATA. I don't care if I never get married.

SUNITA. Just cause you don't care. I wish somebody would do something for me.

MRS WATUMAL. I'm doing – why do you think I went to see Burmawalla?

SUNITA. Great isn't it – go to see the horoscope.

MRS WATUMAL. It's very important to see if there is any moonj, which planets are deterring you from getting married.

MR WATUMAL. You're very fussy. Plain girls of mature age without good dowries can't afford to be fussy.

MOHAN. She's too foul tempered – who's going to marry her?

MRS WATUMAL. Of course she'll be married. I consulted Burmawalla about her bad temper. She must observe eight Tuesday fasts and temper will calm down.

LATA. She's depressed. All she wants is a man.

MOHAN. She thinks Prince Charming is going to come down on a horse and take her! Just like in her Mills and Boons!

SUNITA. Just because you're happy to be a spinster and sit here rotting doesn't mean I am . . .

LATA. I'd rather be a spinster than . . .

MRS WATUMAL. Nobody is going to be a spinster. We are trying to arrange marriages. Matchmaker is coming next week.

SUNITA. Oh that weirdo.

LATA. Sunita's depressed.

SUNITA. Don't speak for me. I'm not bloody depressed.

LATA. You are depressed. Why do you stuff your guts all the time?

MRS WATUMAL. Oh stop squabbling! This is going to kill me soon.

SUNITA. You're not exactly 'Slim Jim' are you?

MOHAN. You spend all your time arguing instead of using constructive energy. Rest your brains.

MR WATUMAL. And tu nikomo? – All you do is rest. Can't even mend that table.

MOHAN. It's good as new. I've used a special bonding – holds so tight it'll never break.

LATA. If you'd have gone to work we'd have replaced the furniture with new furniture instead of bonding it together.

MOHAN. You wait – I'll replace the whole flat – the whole building.

MR WATUMAL. Sheik Chilli – that's what he is.

LATA (*showing a newspaper advertisement*). Papa – please look at this.

MR WATUMAL. Where – what is it?

LATA. 'Telephone operator and receptionist required by Oberoi Hotel'. Let me apply for it.

MR WATUMAL. You can't work in the hotel. I can't have people telling me that my daughters are supporting me.

LATA. I want to work.

SUNITA. Papa don't let her work in the hotel. I've heard some horrendous stories.

LATA. They're good jobs Papa. They're lots of people who are college educated in these places.

MR WATUMAL. Once you are married you do anything.

SUNITA. Men in hotels want only one thing from a girl. And it isn't marriage.

MRS WATUMAL. And how will you marry before your sister? People will say there is something wrong with her that the younger is marrying before the elder.

LATA. And if Sunita never marries am I just to sit here rotting all my life?

SUNITA. You're so selfish – can't you at least wait until my marriage is arranged? Then you do what you want.

LATA. Who's talking about marriage? I want to work.

MR WATUMAL. You are so adamant you want to work. I have a very good suggestion. This 'Sonny Jim' doesn't want to take the responsibility in the factory. You come there and help me.

LATA. Papa that's not work.

MRS WATUMAL. Go and help your father. That way you can work and people will talk but not so much and not so bad.

SUNITA. And who's going to do all the housework round here?

MR WATUMAL. You can help your mother.

MOHAN. Yeh – go and make yourself useful for once.

MR WATUMAL. OK beta. That's settled. From tomorrow you come to the factory.


## Scene Nine

*We move to the* PUMNANI*s' flat. Time has passed – it is about a week later making it 22nd March. Early evening.* MRS HATHIRAMANI *and* MRS BHAGWANDAS *have come to see* REKHA *and* PUPHI.

REKHA. Will you have something?

MRS HATHIRAMANI. Not for me – you know my problem with Shani. Today is Saturday and Bahi Sahib says I must observe the fast.

REKHA. Jashoti?

MRS BHAGWANDAS. Na Rekha.

MRS HATHIRAMANI. Last week I bought this sapphire from P.B. Bhau – it is touching my skin, so hopefully now everything will be all right.

REKHA. Chungo, now what can I do for you?

MRS BHAGWANDAS. I think we have found somebody for our Lakshmi.

MRS HATHIRAMANI. Yes. That's why we are here today, to tell you about –

MRS BHAGWANDAS. Hari. His name is Hari.

MRS HATHIRAMANI. Samtani.

MRS BHAGWANDAS. You know the Samtani's of course?

MRS HATHIRAMANI. They are Amils – educated.

MRS BHAGWANDAS. Of course they are in Bhaibund occupation now.

MRS HATHIRAMANI. But who isn't doing Bhaibund trade in Bombay these days? In Bombay you see the things have changed.

MRS BHAGWANDAS. Suitcases. They have a shop in Mahim. They will be expanding after the boy's wedding.

MRS HATHIRAMANI. Anyway, originally they are Amil. The way you wanted it.

MRS BHAGWANDAS. The boy is educated.

MRS HATHIRAMANI. B.A. Commerce passed.

REKHA. Well it is Kishin's wish to have an educated son in law.

MRS HATHIRAMANI. He is the only boy.

MRS BHAGWANDAS. No other children so our Lakshmi will be treated very well. Hari will inherit everything – there is a nice bungalow there.

MRS HATHIRAMANI. And of course Lakshmi means Goddess of Wealth so whatever house she enters will be prosperous.

PUPHI. What is his colouring?

MRS BHAGWANDAS. Colour is dark.

MRS HATHIRAMANI. What is his colour when background is good?

PUPHI. Any defects?

MRS BHAGWANDAS. One eye is not seeing properly but you sit opposite him and his eyes meet yours.

MRS HATHIRAMANI. And we do have a slight problem with dowry.

MRS BHAGWANDAS. Without this defect such a boy from such a family would expect a good offer of dowry. They will be satisfied with minimum.

PUPHI. Dark and defective and still we must offer?

MRS HATHIRAMANI. Not defective – an accident – not at birth so children won't be affected.

PUPHI. You've seen our Lakshmi – she's beautiful, colour is fair – why should we give her to such a boy?

REKHA. I'm a bit worried. Hari is the only child – she'll have to do everything.

MRS HATHIRAMANI. You look at it this way Rekha. If it was a big family she'd have to look after the brothers in law, nanand – everyone.

PUPHI. It's not giving me a nice feeling.

REKHA. I want my daughter to be happy.

MRS HATHIRAMANI. Mukhé kar thri he. You think we'd suggest someone she won't be happy with?

REKHA. You know our circumstances – what can we offer?

MRS HATHIRAMANI. If you do not offer, Lakshmi will lose this chance. She is hitting marriageable age. The boy has so many mitis and there's still Padma to think of. Tell Sham to borrow from somewhere.

MRS BHAGWANDAS. Anyway it is only minimum, not even half sai. And you don't have a mitiwala as a go between bumping up the dowry. They'll expect customary offerings on engagement and the rest of deti-leti Mrs Hathiramani and I will finalise.

MRS HATHIRAMANI. Look, you meet the boy and if things click then we can decide.

MRS BHAGWANDAS. See the boy.

REKHA. Chungo. Lakshmi is now eighteen. I'll talk to Sham – we'll arrange something.

MRS HATHIRAMANI. Yes. That's good. Hullo.

MRS BHAGWANDAS. Han. Ram Ram Rekha.

REKHA. Han Om.

MRS HATHIRAMANI. Han Om Puphi.

*They leave the flat and as lights are fading out on them going back to their respective flats – at the same time lights are coming up on* SHAM *and* RANI *on the terrace.*


**Scene Ten**

*The terrace. There are kites flying in the sky. It is dusk. We can also hear the noise off the street below.* SHAM *is there and* RANI *comes up.*

RANI. Hi.

SHAM. Oh hi.

RANI. Such a lovely breeze.

SHAM. Mmmm.

RANI. You come up here a lot.

SHAM. And you always seem to know when I'm here.

RANI. Well I really enjoy your company. I hope you don't mind me saying that. You know I always feel it's just nice to speak my mind. There's really no one else I can talk to like this. Nobody actually wants to listen to me.

SHAM. Don't exaggerate.

RANI. I'm not.

RANI. How's Lakshmi?

SHAM. She's OK. Mrs Hathiramani and Mrs Bhagwandas have just been round about a boy for her.

RANI. Does she want an arranged marriage?

SHAM. Yeah. Sure.

RANI. Oh God I don't. I definitely want a love marriage. My mother keeps trying to arrange something, but I'm my own person. I have my own ideas – no one is going to tell me anymore what to do.

SHAM. I saw you at the Taj the other day.

RANI. Really?

SHAM. I wanted to come and say hello.

RANI. You should have, yaar.

SHAM. You have a different class of friends than mine.

RANI. What does that mean?

SHAM. You have the freedom to do what you like.

RANI. I don't. You don't know what it's like at home. My mother has to dominate everything. I can't even decorate my room the way I want it.

SHAM. But you have such a lovely home.

RANI. It's awful. It's so showy. My mother wants people to know how much money we have. If you have money and everyone knows it, why do you have to show it?

SHAM. You're such a spoilt little madam, aren't you.

RANI. But I feel trapped at home. Look at your sisters – they're so lucky – they can take a bus wherever they want to – they really live.

SHAM. Poor little rich girl – can't take a bus.

RANI. I'm serious. Once I made my ayah take me on a bus and my mother blew a fit – she gave me a real beating for it.

SHAM. What's the big deal about travelling on a bus? – full of men trying to get fresh with you. Look we don't have any of the things you have. I don't even know how I'm going to offer for Lakshmi.

RANI. God it's tacky the way we Sindhi's are so materialistic.

SHAM. Well I have to find a dowry – my parents can't do anything.

RANI. Why don't you borrow? When you have a job you can pay it back.

SHAM. With my reputation my job prospects aren't brilliant and your father isn't going to give me a glowing reference.

RANI. Well I don't believe for a second you're a thief. Oh look there's Gopal.

GOPAL *is downstairs – he comes into focus.*

Wave to him. I really tease him. I tease him and Raju a lot you know.

SHAM. How?

RANI. I just wave to them and they think I really like them.

*He laughs.*

They do. The best is when I stand in the lift. I stand there very quietly and just as I'm about to get off at my floor I turn around and smile at him. You should see his face. Even better is Pinky in the lift – my God yaar – she touched Gopal's arse the other day – so disgusting.

**Scene Eleven**

*Through this scene lights gradually fade on* SHAM *and* RANI *on the terrace.* RAJU *and* GOPAL *playing jacks, and discussing the game in Hindi.*

GOPAL. Hey look up there.

RAJU. Kya?

GOPAL. That sala thief. He's pestering a weak girl.

RAJU. Kaun? Chun Chun. (*Wiggling his bum.*)

GOPAL. Yeah – Murli's girl. He's telling her to run away with him.

RAJU. How do you know?

GOPAL. Their eyes meet, their hands touch and he . . .

RAJU. What happens?

GOPAL. Na – you're too young.

RAJU. What like this? (*Sticking his tongue out.*)

GOPAL. Salé where did you see that? I'm going to tell your mother.

RAJU. I saw it on television when my memsahib was asleep. The hero was doing it to the girl.

GOPAL. My lottery's about to come up – when I tell your father that thief does his posing upstairs and leads her astray I'll really earn some hard cash. I'll take you to the hotel and feed you chicken tikka.

RAJU. Chicken tikka?

GOPAL. Well I've seen them three times now – might even be able to take in a picture. I'll get tickets on black. Front row seats.

HOSHIAR SINGH *passes them on his way out of the building.*

GOPAL. Késé hein Hoshiar Singh?

HOSHIAR SINGH. Chalta hé. Murjani Sahib is having twenty guests for dinner – as usual no notice so now I have to go and get crate of soda for their negronis.

GOPAL. What's the occasion?

HOSHIAR SINGH. Ganesh pooja for the nephew's engagement, but you know what they're like – after they've had their prashad they like to get drunk.

HOSHIAR SINGH *exits.*

GOPAL. Here have a beedi – I've got plenty. Sala, without the wages from your father – where would we be – take one and don't tell Mrs Hathi – she'll put her evil eye on me.

**Scene Twelve**

*The HATHIRAMANI flat. Nine days have passed. It is 1st April – Sindhi New Year. Early evening – MRS HATHIRAMANI enters the flat. Sound of lift arriving.*

MR HATHIRAMANI. 'Arrivals' – 6 pm. Wife . . . 'Comments' – return from Crawford Market.

MRS HATHIRAMANI *(calling)*. Hedan, I am back. I have taken the dekchi of offering to Nariman Point for Saint Jhulelal and I've brought some lovely fresh fish for you. *(She shows it to him.)*

MRS HATHIRAMANI. Hedan, desso desso.

MR HATHIRAMANI. Get it out of here. All you do is disturb my work.

MRS HATHIRAMANI. I will fry the fish with spices. Also I will fry some aubergine and make some daal and tonight even I will have a piece of fish.

MR HATHIRAMANI. Why do you call yourself vegetarian?

MRS HATHIRAMANI. Fish is not non veg on Sindhi New Years. Even for vegetarians, it is permitted.

MR HATHIRAMANI. I am in the midst of translation of our Sind's immortal poet, Shah Abdul Latif and I must not be disturbed.

MRS HATHIRAMANI. For food shall I call you? Or do you wish also now to fast for your work.

MR HATHIRAMANI. Call me. (MRS HATHIRAMANI *goes back to front room.*) Raju Raju!

MRS HATHIRAMANI. Come on Raju – up you get. Take down the old lime and chillies and put up the new one.

RAJU (*he gets up*). Memsahib I will fall.

MRS HATHIRAMANI. Gaddah! You climb those trees across the road quicker than a monkey.

RAJU. Memsahib – you are hurting me.

MRS HATHIRAMANI. You, Mua, just keep still and tie it there. (*He does.*)

MRS HATHIRAMANI. I have burnt the chillies that Mataji gave me and there was no smell. This proves the evil eye is upon us. Tie it tightly. Now no evil is passing through this door. Now get down and bring me that piece of alum that I put on the coals. (*He gets it.*) Tonight – no going out with your friends.

RAJU. But you know there's a servant's cricket match. I'm in the team.

MRS HATHIRAMANI. If you don't play for one day what will happen? That Gopal fellow is teaching you all the wrong things. You should learn what's good for you. Where does he sleep? Near the lift. Where do you sleep? Inside the house. We let you sleep in the passage, don't we?

RAJU. I'll sleep outside.

MRS HATHIRAMANI. To wander around at night! Mr Hathiramani – he needs anything at night – you have to be here.

RAJU. Always I have to wake up in the night.

MRS HATHIRAMANI. You have to work for your food – where were you living before? In that jupatpati. And where do you live now? In this nice building Sadhbela. And tonight what will you be eating?– fresh fish – the same as your Sahib and I. Now separate the fruit I've bought. (*She goes in to* MR HATHIRAMANI.)

Buddo te – I'll show you something – you wouldn't believe me – Dessote  – what does it look like to you?

MR HATHIRAMANI. That is nothing. Take your superstitious nonsense out of here.

MRS HATHIRAMANI. Look don't quarrel with me today. If you begin the month quarrelling we will be quarrelling the whole of the month.

MR HATHIRAMANI. Sayon dhi buckbuck pie kari!

MRS HATHIRAMANI. Your Hyderbadi superiority won't let you believe. Mataji said you burn this thing and then you will see who is against you.

MR HATHIRAMANI. And you did it. You are from Rohri – this is why you are so stupid. Why do you waste your time going to this Mataji? Go to Unnati Mandal. Work with your Sindhi sisters. They are doing good charity work for the poor Sindhis in Ulhasnagar. You should educate yourself.

MRS HATHIRAMANI. Your education has made you blind. Look, it is a face – that is a nose and those are the eyes.

MR HATHIRAMANI. That can look like anything. If I want it to look like a papaya it can look like a papaya – if I want it to look like an ananas it can look like an ananas – where will your ignorance lead you?

MRS HATHIRAMANI. It is not a papaya. It's a face. And look at this nose. Who in Sadhbela has a nose like this? I will tell you. It is Mrs Watumal.

MR HATHIRAMANI. So you think Mrs Watumal is doing all this?

MRS HATHIRAMANI. Yes and you know why. They were trying to arrange their good for nothing son with your cousin's daughter and you told your cousin not to.

MR HATHIRAMANI. Yes because of my findings of that boy Mohan – it's all in here.

MRS HATHIRAMANI. And now Mrs Watumal is doing this to us.

MR HATHIRAMANI. Doing what? I don't believe in all this.

MRS HATHIRAMANI. Yes when you believe in it – I am here to save you. (MRS HATHIRAMANI *returns to the kitchen.*) Raju, prepare the masala for the fish. One bottle of Thumbs Up drink is missing from the crate.

RAJU. Memsahib, last night you had indigestion – at one o'clock in the morning you got up and drank it yourself.

MRS HATHIRAMANI. Don't answer me back. (*Calling to* MR HATHIRAMANI.) Budothe – I met Mrs Samtani at Crawford Market – they have decided to accept Lakshmi.

MR HATHIRAMANI. Well that's something useful you've done – they won't be sorry.

MRS HATHIRAMANI. So how was the meeting of the co-operative?

MR HATHIRAMANI. We discussed the Murjani's extension – we completely blocked his plans. Sadhbela will not take the weight nor the extra evacuation of water and waste.

MRS HATHIRAMANI. Aah.

MR HATHIRAMANI. As it is his extra toilet is causing leakage in Watumal's kitchen.

MRS HATHIRAMANI. Han. How can they cook? Well Murli is trying to show off his money.

MR HATHIRAMANI. It was agreed unanimously and it tanta-mounted to the fact that he can't have an extension. Also he must repair the pipes that are troubling Mr Watumal in his kitchen.

MRS HATHIRAMANI. Chungo. No one can go above your head. After all without you, there would be no Sadhbela. Raju put some more chilli.

MR HATHIRAMANI. Then Mr Bhagwandas proposed that I read them an extract of my work. They know that I'm preparing an archive of the exiled Hindu Sindhi.

MRS HATHIRAMANI. What is archive?

MR HATHIRAMANI. Library.

MRS HATHIRAMANI. See your sahib is educated.

RAJU. Memsahib – send me also for education.

MRS HATHIRAMANI. Where have you seen a servant going to school? Now cut this aubergine.

MR HATHIRAMANI. Our heritage is in disarray. Nowhere in India can the Sindhis speak their own language – in Punjab there is Punjabi – in Gujerat, Gujerati but where is the Sind that we can speak our beloved Sindhi? People are crazy because they think English is the international language therefore they are only thinking of internationality and not of their own nationality. That's the pity. Not only have we lost our homeland but we are fast losing our culture. With the dispersal of Sindhis all over the world in pursuit of wealth it is inevitable.

MRS HATHIRAMANI. Yes.

MR HATHIRAMANI. Even in the camps we had our own recitals, poetry readings – now who has heard of our great Sufi poet – Shah Abdul Latif? Even Bhagwandas Bhau had forgotten him.

MRS HATHIRAMANI. You were a journalist in Sind. That is why you know these things.

MR HATHIRAMANI. Like everyone he is too busy making money. He has a perfectly good name like Pitambar and he changes it to P.B. He thinks he's very modern – he has time only for business not his culture.

MRS HATHIRAMANI. Yes.

MR HATHIRAMANI. The message of Latif's work is essential in this world of material values. Leila was so tempted by a diamond necklace worth nine lakhs of rupees that she sold a night with her husband to the daughter of a Hindu Prince. But, as Latif points out, what she thought was a necklace became a stone around her neck.

RAJU. Memsahib aubergines are cut.

MR HATHIRAMANI. 'Aero zayver vija baahay munj, eh haar pitto khariyan khaddo munj.' 'Fain would I fling, the ornament in the oven the necklace in the ditch'.

MRS HATHIRAMANI. OK so clean the fish now.

MR HATHIRAMANI. 'Oven' – tell me another word for oven.

MRS HATHIRAMANI. Oven is oven. I only know one word for each thing. I don't confuse myself with many words.

MR HATHIRAMANI. I need another word for oven.

MRS HATHIRAMANI. Why do you need another word for oven? You are only heating up your brains unnecessarily.

MR HATHIRAMANI. When I translate Abdul Latif's poetry I can't use a small word like oven. There must be a word.

RAJU. Kiln.

MRS HATHIRAMANI. You shut up. Let me taste the masala.

MR HATHIRAMANI. Aatcha Raju. Bring the dictionary.

MRS HATHIRAMANI. I'll bring it – what does he know about dictionaries?

RAJU. Memsahib – masala.

MRS HATHIRAMANI. He has made good masala.

MR HATHIRAMANI. Brazier, furnace. Oven.

MRS HATHIRAMANI. No, salt is not enough.

## Scene Thirteen

*We move outside Sadhbela to the* SAMTANI's *flat in Mahim.*
LAKSHMI *is now married to* HARI. *It is about five weeks later
round about 7th May. Late evening.* LAKSHMI *is folding away
some clothes.*

MRS SAMTANI. No gharan dharan – bed, cupboard, rasai,
pillows, nothing for the house. You came sari mein.

LAKSHMI. We gave the refrigerator and clothes.

MRS SAMTANI. Nylon saris, not Japanese silk and some of
Hari's aunts still haven't received.

LAKSHMI. But you knew I would be coming with minimum.

MRS SAMTANI. Minimum doesn't mean nothing. Even
reception was in a temple yard. Paper plates – no Sindhi
kadhi, no boondi, not even a movie of the wedding and then
the drinks ran out – can you imagine my embarrassment
when the guests started leaving?

LAKSHMI. Sham borrowed. He did the best he could. He gave
cash settlement.

MRS SAMTANI. Buddé Devki – that was only the first
instalment – we explained to you the need to expand our
business. Tell Sham he must settle in full.

LAKSHMI. If there is anything left to settle, Sham will pay.

MRS SAMTANI. I've been so kind to you – I let Hari take you
to Bangalore for your honeymoon – you have privacy in this
house but your family have not fulfilled their side.

LAKSHMI. Let me talk to them.

MRS SAMTANI. You think I'm asking for myself – I'm
thinking of your children.

HARI *enters.*

MRS SAMTANI. Hello puther. How was business today?

HARI. Good. So how are the two women in my life?

MRS SAMTANI. I've been showing Devki how we do things
here. She's not yet used to being a wife.

HARI. Well mama – I've given her strict instructions – I hope she's looking after you.

MRS SAMTANI. She does things very differently.

HARI. You learn to please my mother, you'll please me and we'll all be happy.

MRS SAMTANI. Devki, get Hari whatever he wants – I'll leave you two youngsters alone.

*She goes.*

LAKSHMI. So you had a good day?

HARI. Hari. There's a lot of interest in our overnight range.

LAKSHMI. That's good.

*Pause.*

HARI. What did you do today?

LAKSHMI. Oh this and that – housework.

HARI. You and Mama getting on all right?

LAKSHMI. She still calls me Devki – she knows I don't like it.

HARI. Give her time. She'll stop doing it.

LAKSHMI. But Hari – my name's Lakshmi – I only changed my name at the wedding because the pandit said to – you promised me no one would call me Devki.

HARI. What's the harm? Why create conflict?

*Pause.*

LAKSHMI. Have you eaten? Can I get you anything?

HARI. No I called out for something.

LAKSHMI. Sure?

HARI. I'm lucky to have a wife to look after me.

LAKSHMI. Are you really happy with me?

HARI. Of course I am.

LAKSHMI. I don't think your mother's so happy.

HARI. Why? Everything's going all right in the house?

LAKSHMI. Well I do the work but she never seems satisfied.

HARI. Try harder.

LAKSHMI. I'm trying but it's so difficult.

HARI. Then you can't be doing things the way she wants them.

LAKSHMI. I don't know what she wants. Everything I do is wrong.

HARI. Give her time. She's not used to having another woman in the house.

LAKSHMI. I'm also finding it hard to settle in a new home.

HARI. You lived in two rooms with six people and you're telling me you can't adjust to one person.

LAKSHMI. Hari, can't you talk to her?

HARI. You're criticising my mother – what position are you putting me in?– you want me to fight with my own mother?

LAKSHMI. No of course not – but she's saying things which aren't true.

HARI. What are you saying? I come home and what do you tell me – things against my mother.

LAKSHMI. She says we haven't settled in full, but I know Sham paid what was due.

HARI. Oh come on – be fair – you came with nothing – we couldn't even have a display.

LAKSHMI. You knew we were poor – you knew our background.

HARI. We didn't know anything. Your father was a headmaster and produced a bloody thief – your family kept that well hidden.

LAKSHMI. Sham's got a job now – that's all behind him.

HARI. He's working for that goonda Akbar Ali – what sort of job is that?

LAKSHMI. Hari, please don't insult my brother. I want to live here happily.

48

HARI. If you want to live here happily, tell them to pay in full, respect my mother.

LAKSHMI *lies down on the bed and* HARI *comes beside her and takes her forcefully.*


**Scene Fourteen**

*The* MURJANI*'s sea-facing flat on the seventh floor. It's one week later – 14th May. Lunch. The diamond setters are there.* HOSHIAR SINGH, *the servant, is serving lunch.*

MRS MURJANI. Hi darling! Come and have lunch. Hoshiar Singh! Choti Memsahib ke liyé plate lao! So, how was college?

RANI. OK.

MRS MURJANI. OK? So what's the long face for, only OK?

RANI. College is college. What do you want?

MRS MURJANI. I can't believe I'm hearing this. Do you know the fight I put up to get Papa to let you go to college.

RANI. Yes I know. I know you've done all that for me Ma. But something's not right.

MRS MURJANI. Well darling, I was saying you needn't go to college if you didn't want to.

RANI. No I want to go to college but I mean I'm going to graduate soon and I want to do something. I just want to organise my mind.

MRS MURJANI. Darling you just concentrate on getting your B.A. and then we'll organise your mind for you. How's that?

RANI. What does that mean now?

MRS MURJANI. Well we'll settle you down.

RANI. You always bring this up about settling down. I don't want to settle down.

MRS MURJANI. Sweetheart! Sweetheart – don't get upset.

RANI. Don't sweetheart me.

MRS MURJANI. I'm only trying to talk to you.

*Silence.*

MRS MURJANI. Come on, have a chapati. Hoshiar Singh!
Garam chapati lao!

RANI. I'm not hungry.

MRS MURJANI. Have some curry at least – I've had Hoshiar
Singh make it specially.

RANI. I'm just not hungry, OK.

MRS MURJANI. Darling, you've become so ill-mannered.
Sweetheart, come and have lunch with me, I hardly ever see
you.

RANI. Talk and I'm listening.

MRS MURJANI. Sweetie, you really oughn't to wear this tee
shirt.

RANI. You always start on me! Just leave it ma.

MRS MURJANI. Darling I'll take you shopping. We'll go
shopping on Saturday.

RANI. I don't want to go shopping. I like being the way I am.
You're always trying to change me.

MRS MURJANI. I'm not criticising. I'm just saying these tee
shirts look really rather cheap. OK don't worry you wear
what you want.

RANI. Mom!

MRS MURJANI. Listen – I want you to come with me on
Saturday. I've got tickets for The Sakhi Samelen ball. And
please sweetheart you'll wear something desi for me, won't
you?

RANI. OK OK I'll wear a sari – so they all know I'm ready to
be married.

MRS MURJANI. Sweetie please don't be difficult.

RANI. Oh come on mom, we all know these balls are only there
to get us all hitched.

MRS MURJANI. Why do you shy away from Sindhi boys?
We're just trying to get you youngsters together.

RANI. Just leave it mom.

MRS MURJANI. Darling, I'm really glad you came home for lunch, because I want you to tell me something. I'm sure it can't possibly be true – I know my daughter, but I have been hearing rumours. Now, were you at the Taj on Tuesday afternoon with Pinky Lalwani, Sushu and some boys?

RANI. Yaar – so?

MRS MURJANI. Yaar so – you were hanging round the Taj with boys – I don't believe this and on top of this I have to hear these things from the likes of Mrs Watumal spreading rumours in Sadhbela.

RANI. What did I do wrong? I was just sitting there drinking coffee.

MRS MURJANI. Drinking coffee with boys – why can't you tell me – why can't you come to me and say Mummy –

RANI. Because if I came to you – you wouldn't let me go – Pinky's mother doesn't do that –

MRS MURJANI. Don't Pinky this and Pinky that!

RANI. Why not?

MRS MURJANI. Because that girl just doesn't come into the conversation.

RANI. That girl is my friend.

MRS MURJANI. OK she's your friend but Mrs Lalwani is a very bad influence, and as far as Sushu goes – she's a Shikarpuri and you know if I look down on the Bhaibunds I look even further down on the Shikarpuris. I don't want you mixing with them.

RANI. Don't be such a snob, Ma.

MRS MURJANI. Now you just listen to me – Mr Watumal was nothing more than a rag and bone man going round selling China in Sind and Mrs Watumal always trying to copy my taste. And now I have to listen to them that my daughter . . .

RANI. Don't listen to these rumours then. You care more about what Mrs Watumal says. Why don't you listen to what I have to say?

MRS MURJANI. I keep telling your papa – why don't we move out of Sadhbela – we have the money but your papa won't have it.

RANI. Look I sat at the Taj. I spoke to Iqbal, I spoke to Girish, I spoke to Pinky – what is wrong?

MRS MURJANI. Iqbal, Girish – who are they?

RANI. Iqbal – Trojan Toothbrushes Girish – Enjay Engineering.

MRS MURJANI. Who are they to you?

RANI. Oh mother they are my friends.

MRS MURJANI. Sweetie, I don't mind you going out in a crowd but three boys and three girls is just not done. If you've got someone in mind why don't you come to me and say Mummy there's a boy I like. Your Papa and I are very liberal.

RANI. I don't – want to marry any of them.

MRS MURJANI. There is such a thing as a reputation, young lady. Sweetie – I have to go out this afternoon. Your mummy's giving an interview to 'The Illustrated' – they're doing an article on the wives of prominent businessmen. I want you to keep an eye on the diamonds, sweetie.

RANI. No I can't – I'm going out.

MRS MURJANI. You're not going anywhere – this is your study period – you seem to have forgotten madam that it was me who fought with Papa to make sure that you went to college.

RANI. I wish you hadn't done it now because after I finish college you're not going to let me do anything. (*She cries.*)

MRS MURJANI. Oh stop whingeing. I'm an M.A. Papa's only a B.A. – I understood that you needed to study.

RANI. You just want to get me married.

MRS MURJANI. No one's going to make you marry.

RANI. I want a career. I want to do social work.

HOSHIAR SINGH. Car's ready Memsahib.

MRS MURJANI. OK, You tell the driver Memsahib will be five minutes. Come on sweetheart. I have to go. Cheer up – you have to keep a watch on the diamonds.

RANI. I don't care about your diamonds.

MRS MURJANI. They're not my diamonds – I'm having them set for you.

RANI. You're having them set for my marriage. I don't want them set.

MRS MURJANI. I'm having them set today – doesn't mean I'm marrying you off tomorrow. You can't get a trousseau together overnight.

HOSHIAR SINGH. Madam, car is waiting.

MRS MURJANI. You just tell him to wait. How much do I pay him every month?– Don't come and pester me.

I'm going now. OK sweetheart? You just study. If you get hungry there's plenty more curry in the fridge. OK I'll see you later darling. Give Mummy a kiss. See you darling.

MRS MURJANI *leaves her flat and takes the lift to the ground floor. As she get out she meets* LAKSHMI.

MRS MURJANI. Hello Lakshmi. How are you?

LAKSHMI. Fine thank you auntie.

MRS MURJANI. You've really blossomed – married life must agree with you. Give my best to your mother.

LAKSHMI *goes up the stairs. She enters the* PUMNANI *flat. She is carrying a bundle of her possessions.*

LAKSHMI. Namasté Ama.

REKHA. Lakshmi, we weren't expecting you. What is this?

LAKSHMI. I've brought my things – I want to come home.

REKHA. What are you saying? Have things got no better?

LAKSHMI. Mrs Samtani is still saying that Sham hasn't settled in full.

REKHA. Beta – Sham went and explained – all that was promised was given.

LAKSHMI. She says it's only an instalment.

53

REKHA. Lakshmi, Sham has no money. Already what he has borrowed he'll be paying off forever – if our circumstances change, then of course we can give a little bit more.

LAKSHMI. They're saying we've deceived them.

PUPHI. Lakshmi – they're liars themselves. Have you seen their house? – a little flat in Mahim somewhere. They don't even have their own car – they're just as poor as we are.

REKHA. What does Hari say?

LAKSHMI. He says what she says.

REKHA. Are you happy with him?

PUPHI. Has he proved himself?

REKHA. Puphi, please.

LAKSHMI. He was kind to me in Bangalore but now he always sides with his mother.

PUPHI. It's the mother in law. See, I told you – you wanted to arrange everything fast. You wanted it all quickly quickly done.

LAKSHMI. Let me come back home mama.

REKHA. How can you come back here? – that is your home now.

LAKSHMI. It's not a home mama.

REKHA. You have to make it your home.

LAKSHMI. Please let me come back mama.

REKHA. It's out of the question. They will use it to get rid of you and if Hari divorces you your life will be ruined.

PUPHI. Sometimes the unbearable must be born.

LAKSHMI *retches.*

REKHA. Beta what's the matter?

LAKSHMI. Nothing.

REKHA *and* PUPHI *exchange a look.*

PUPHI. Good you have got yourself with child.

REKHA. I'll get Sham to go over to the Samtanis and talk to them. Now you are pregnant they must not make you work so hard.

PUPHI. See God has a way of resolving everything – now your place there is secure.

LAKSHMI. No! It's made things worse.

PUPHI. Sab theek thivendo. A child always changes things.

REKHA. You'll eat with us tonight and I'll get Sham to take you home.

LAKSHMI. Ama please I can't go back there.

REKHA. There is no other way.

LAKSHMI. Ama.

REKHA. Don't get upset beta. Things will be all right.


**Scene Sixteen**

*Back in the* SAMTANI's *flat at Mahim. It is two days later – 16th May.*

MRS SAMTANI. Devki is in the bathroom. Everyday she's been vomiting.

DR AGARWAL. Well first few months of pregnancy are always difficult.

MRS SAMTANI. The girl is too delicate. I was doing housework right up to the day Hari was born. My mother in law wouldn't let me rest.

DR AGARWAL. OK I'm ready now.

MRS SAMTANI. Let me call her. Devki – come on Doctor Agarwal is waiting.

LAKSHMI *enters.*

DR AGARWAL. So Devki – how are you feeling?

LAKSHMI. I get very bad nausea but otherwise I'm fine.

55

DR AGARWAL. It's only natural. Come – let's have our checkup. I'm just going to ask you to lie down – relax a little and I'll check the baby.

LAKSHMI. Will it hurt?

DR AGARWAL. No. No, there's no need to be scared is there Mrs Samtani?

MR SAMTANI. Dr Agarwal is the best doctor in Mahim.

DR AGARWAL. I've been doing this for years – come, lie down. Now this isn't going to hurt at all. Mrs Samtani!

LAKSHMI. No I don't need a doctor.

MRS SAMTANI. Lie down Devki.

DR AGARWAL. Ready now?

MR SAMTANI. Come on Devki.

DR AGARWAL. Just checking to see if the baby's all right, Mrs Samtani!

LAKSHMI. No!

DR AGARWAL. Hold her down now!

LAKSHMI *screams. Blackout.*

*Interval.*

## ACT TWO

### Scene Seventeen

*It is the next day – 17th May. Saturday lunchtime. The seafront-dhobis etc are set on stage washing their clothes and others performing ablutions.*

RANI. I have something to tell you. Let's go beyond the dhobi ghat. It's not very private here.

SHAM. What's the matter?

RANI. Nothing's the matter. My head is swimming round just now.

SHAM. Rani, I've got to eat something soon.

RANI. I know you're hungry – you've just come from work.

SHAM. What is it?

RANI. It's not that easy. Just give me a chance. I just wish everything could be more simple you know. I don't know why life has to be so complicated. I spoke to Pinky about it – because I told her I was very embarrassed and I didn't know how to say anything to you and she just said to come right out and tell you. But I'm here and I'm not saying anything.

SHAM. Rani, you're not making any sense.

RANI. I – oh look at that poor woman. I really wish I could help her. I have the money to do it and everything – I mean where do I start? Do you think I'm pretentious? You don't think I'm pretentious do you?

SHAM. No.

RANI. Good. Oh God I can't stand the smell – it's so filthy here.

SHAM. Well let's go back then.

RANI. No come a bit further down. I really have to talk to you.

SHAM. What is it Rani?

RANI. Well – uh – I don't know how to say this. (*She grabs him and kisses him.*)

SHAM. Rani – what are you doing?

RANI. I . . . I . . . Oh God . . .

SHAM. What if somebody saw us?

RANI. I don't care. You're not angry are you?

SHAM. Look I've got to get back.

RANI. Sham I love you. I asked Pinky.

SHAM. You don't know what you're saying.

RANI. I do – I love you. Don't treat me like a child. (*She starts crying.*)

SHAM. Don't cry Rani.

RANI. You don't have to fight your feelings you know – there's no one here.

SHAM. We come from different worlds Rani.

RANI. I don't care – I love you – you're not like the other Sindhi boys I meet. Don't you like me even a little bit?

MRS MURJANI (*from offstage*). Rani, Rani sweetheart – Mummy's here.

RANI. Oh shit it's my mother!

MRS MURJANI. What's wrong sweetheart – why has he brought you down here?

RANI. Oh God how I hate you – why can't you leave me alone?

MRS MURJANI. What are you doing with my daughter?

RANI. He's not doing anything.

MRS MURJANI. I saw from your papa's binoculars what he was up to. Throwing himself on you like that!

RANI. He didn't throw himself on me.

SHAM. Mrs Murjani we were just talking – nothing happened.

MRS MURJANI. I saw what I saw.

RANI. If anyone did it was me.

MR HATHIRAMANI *arrives.*

MR HATHIRAMANI. Mrs Murjani, is everything all right?

RANI. Oh shit.

MR HATHIRAMANI. I came as quickly as I could.

MRS MURJANI. Everything is under control. We don't need
your help. Come on Rani – let's get home now.

MR HATHIRAMANI (*following*). Mrs Murjani. I must speak
with you – it is a matter of the utmost urgency.

MRS MURJANI. Mr Hathiramani – if you don't mind – I would
like to get my daughter home.

MR HATHIRAMANI. Madam – I've been following this boy
and his movements.

MRS MURJANI. So what – what's that to me?

MR HATHIRAMANI. Madam, it has become obvious to me
that he has designs on your daughter.

MRS MURJANI. You have been following this boy and his
movements and you've said nothing to me?

MR HATHIRAMANI. I did not want to accuse unjustly without
sufficient evidence.

RANI. Oh ma – don't listen to him – he's just being nosy.

MRS MURJANI. You just mind your manners madam.

MR HATHIRAMANI. I have noted in my diary seven sightings
both on the terrace and in the lift.

MRS MURJANI. Seven – seven times – what were you doing?
She's a young girl! You should know better. You stay away
from her.

SHAM. Mrs Murjani.

MRS MURJANI. You think you can spoil her so that I would
have no choice but to marry her off to you. My husband tried
to help you – got you a job in Japan and this is how you
repay us. Come on darling.

RANI. Ma!

*They exit.*

MR HATHIRAMANI. Well young man I gave you the benefit of the doubt but now you have shown your true colours.

MR HATHIRAMANI *exits.* SHAM *is left alone on stage – we then follow him back to Sadhbela. As he enters the building he bumps into* LATA WATUMAL.

**Scene Eighteen**

SHAM *and* LATA *in front of the lift. There is also the sound of wedding bands in the streets.* GOPAL *is on his stool.*

LATA. Hi.

SHAM. Hi.

LATA. Don't you recognise me? I'm Lata – Lata Watumal – have I become that fat and ugly that you don't recognise me? I have. (*Laughs.*)

SHAM. No. No, of course not.

LATA. You look terrible – what's happened?

SHAM. Nothing serious – just had a bit of a run in with Mrs Murjani.

LATA. I wouldn't let that female bother you – she's always gossiping about me being twenty nine and not married. Who cares!

Mama tells me you've got a new job.

SHAM. Yes with Akbar Ali.

LATA. Oh.

SHAM. I know you people think he's a smuggler.

LATA. No. No, I didn't mean that at all.

SHAM. No you don't have to be embarrassed – everyone has that reaction. Akbar has nothing to hide – he's no longer involved in that sort of thing – What I'm working on is strictly legit.

LATA. Look I'm sorry. I didn't mean to offend you.

SHAM. No no you haven't – it's just one gets fed up with people jumping to conclusions. Akbar Ali was the only one in town to give me a second chance.

LATA. That's great. I'm also working.

SHAM. Oh really?

LATA. Yah – in Papa's factory. It's good, I'm really enjoying it. I'm trying to update the operation, the whole thing's running down – going to waste.

SHAM. There should be great potential there. You know we're doing a similar turn around with Rebotco Mills.

LATA. Oh – would you do me a favour? – would you come and talk to Papa for me. I'm trying to do it all on my own but Papa doesn't take my ideas that seriously. You see he wants Mohan to take over – but you know what he's like – he hasn't changed.

SHAM. I'm not sure that it would do any good. I'll tell you what. I'll have a word to Akbar Ali if you like – I'm not promising anything but you never know – he might have some ideas.

LATA. Oh that'll be great, thanks so much.

SHAM. No problem.

LATA. OK see you.

*She goes on up to her flat.*


**Scene Nineteen**

*The* WATUMAL'*s. Music of wedding bands and firecrackers exploding continues.* LATA *comes in and starts preparing lunch.*

MR WATUMAL. Listen to this band baja.

MRS WATUMAL. Han, gives me a headache.

MR WATUMAL. I pray before I die we'll have band bajas playing, lights strung from our balconies.

MRS WATUMAL. Han.

MR WATUMAL. People getting married having grandchildren.

SUNITA. Oh shut up Papa – it's bad enough that we have to put up with the noise.

MRS WATUMAL. Yes all this noise doesn't help my migraine – it won't go, I can't do anything about it.

MR WATUMAL. You should all be married by now. Mohan, from tomorrow I want you to go and help Lata in the factory. I'm retiring from today.

SUNITA. Good idea.

MOHAN. What do you mean good idea?

MR WATUMAL. Look at me. How old am I? – can't cope anymore.

LATA. Chapatis or rice Papa?

MR WATUMAL. She goes to office – comes back, cooks lunch, goes back – you should be running the factory son.

MRS WATUMAL. Yes.

MOHAN. Papa how many times have I said the factory's useless. You might as well kiss it goodbye.

LATA. What does everyone want?

MRS WATUMAL. You cook rice beta.

LATA. Mohan you should listen to Papa. Our future's in the factory.

MOHAN. You go to the factory two days and you think you know the world.

LATA. Papa, I just bumped into Sham. You know what we're trying in the factory – he's already doing. His boss is putting money into ventures like ours.

MR WATUMAL. Puther – that boy – his reputation is not good.

SUNITA. Papa tell him to stop smoking I can't bear it! He has no respect.

MR WATUMAL. Listen to your sister.

SUNITA. You shouldn't allow him to smoke in front of you.

MR WATUMAL. You waste all the money that you get from me on these cigarettes.

MOHAN. Papa.

MR WATUMAL. You go to the coffee shops – you're wasting your life son.

MOHAN. I'm making creative use of my time. I'm the only son – I've got to work out the future of this family.

MR WATUMAL. Me and your mother should be having grandchildren by now. Sunita you're getting so fat – you should be thickening with children.

SUNITA. Papa don't get excited.

MR WATUMAL. What will happen?

SUNITA. Your blood pressure will go up.

MR WATUMAL. What is my blood pressure . . . ?

MRS WATUMAL. Aiee allah! Don't upset yourself – I'm already sick with my headache.

SUNITA. Oh please, I'm trying to concentrate on this article.

MOHAN. Papa I met this Arab Sheikh yesterday.

MR WATUMAL. Is he going to feed you?

MOHAN. I told him about my Plan Of Action for the Government rest houses. He looked at me and said 'Boy, you've got a very bright future ahead of you.'

MR WATUMAL. Your plans are futile son.

SUNITA. They're just an excuse to sit around in coffee shops spending papa's money.

MR WATUMAL. From tomorrow you're getting no pocket money from me – from anybody.

MOHAN. Papa – you've got to speculate to accumulate. I can earn money like this – I know how business works, I've been in this game long enough. Just let me get this Sheikh on my side and we'll clinch it. Just think how many mouldering rest houses there are all over India. It'll be the happening thing.

MR WATUMAL. If we go bankrupt – who will marry your sisters – who will give you a daughter?

SUNITA. Who is marrying us anyway?

MR WATUMAL. Have you spoken to upstairs? Mr Murjani?

MOHAN. What's the point?

MR WATUMAL. Huh – about the leakage – have you? You can't even do that.

MRS WATUMAL. Yes, you can't even cook in the kitchen.

MR WATUMAL. You take no responsibility in this house, it is falling to pieces. It is up to you now to tell Murjani to do something. It was agreed at the last meeting and still he's done nothing. The Murjanis are just showing off their money, and not thinking how it is affecting other people.

SUNITA. Papa, there's no point asking Mohan to do anything.

MR WATUMAL. This Sadhbela has two young people – that boy upstairs is a thief and my son he wastes his time. You know your mother blames the Hathiramani's for the breakup of your engagement but let me tell you, frankly he spoke the truth – you have a reputation for being an idler.

MOHAN. I never wanted to marry Mr Hathiramani's niece anyway.

MRS WATUMAL. We had the introduction at The Sea Lounge of The Taj Mahal Hotel paying so many rupees for English sandwiches with no taste and bread so thin, and then it comes to nothing.

MOHAN. Mama, she wasn't right. You know I'd much rather go for someone like Padma Pumnani – she's more my type.

MRS WATUMAL. We can't consider the Pumnanis. See how they're living now.

SUNITA. When are we having food? I'm hungry.

MRS WATUMAL. No one's offered me anything to eat – not even a cup of tea.

SUNITA. Lata, Ama's hungry and so am I.

MR WATUMAL. Stop ordering your sister. She's not your servant.

MOHAN. Papa, I promise, this is the last time. I need some money.

MR WATUMAL. I'm not going to give you a single pai.

MOHAN. Ma – please explain to Papa. I just have to take the Sheikh out – dinner or something and introduce him to my other partners.

SUNITA. Don't come and suck up to Mama now.

MOHAN. Shut up!

SUNITA. Mum, he's just trying to suck up to you.

MOHAN. Mum has a weak head – do you understand that? – talking at the top of your voice.

MR WATUMAL. Mohan, come and sit here.

MOHAN. I can hear yaar.

MR WATUMAL. You calling me yaar. I'm your father.

MRS WATUMAL. Respect your father.

MOHAN. Papa we just need to strike one deal and we'll be set for life.

MR WATUMAL. Lata, tomorrow you take Mohan to the factory, you teach him the ropes.

LATA. That's fine by me Papa.

MOHAN. They're so many liabilities – cut your losses and sell it off.

MR WATUMAL. Who will buy it?

LATA. Papa I'm telling you. People are interested – Sham's talking to Akbar Ali.

MOHAN. That bloody joker – All that goonda wants to do is launder his black money and make things look legal.

LATA. This is legitimate business OK.

SUNITA. Papa, can you lend me some money? I want to go for Weight Watchers.

MR WATUMAL. Puther, I have no money.

SUNITA. Papa, I never ask you for anything.

MR WATUMAL. Please don't interrupt – we're talking about the factory.

SUNITA. Nobody cares about me.

MR WATUMAL. Sunita – we all care about you – come on, let's have some lunch now Baba. Come on.


**Scene Twenty**

*The* PUMNANI'*s – seventh floor. A few days have passed. It's Thursday 22nd – afternoon.* SHAM, KISHIN *(in background),* MRS HATHIRAMANI, REKHA, PUPHI *and* PADMA *are all present. Lights come up.*

SWEEPER. Shall I do Kishin Sahib's room now?

PADMA. No he's still asleep – you do there.

SWEEPER *goes and starts sweeping,*

REKHA. You should have let me stay at the hospital.

SHAM. No Mama – there was nothing that you could do. She's had a major operation – It'll be some time.

MRS HATHIRAMANI. You need a rest Rekha.

SHAM. They'll ring us when Lakshmi wakes up.

PADMA: Mummy do you want some tea?

REKHA. No thanks puther. Please make sure that your papa's had his medicines.

PADMA. OK Mummy. Auntie can I get you anything?

MRS HATHIRAMANI. No don't worry. Raju is just coming with the lunch.

REKHA. She should be at home. I should be looking after her.

MRS HATHIRAMANI. She's not in any state.

REKHA. She must be with her mother.

MRS HATHIRAMANI. We must send her quickly to her in laws to recover.

REKHA. She must recover, as is the custom with birth in the house of her mother.

MRS HATHIRAMANI. These are different circumstances. Rekha, it's not a delivery – Doctor said she'd had an abortion.

REKHA. There must be some mistake. Lakshmi phoned me to say she was miscarrying.

*Somewhere here lights up on* RAJU *coming downstairs with tiffin.*

MRS HATHIRAMANI. Did she? Doctor said no. He said it was the usual back street job – very messy.

REKHA. I know my baby. She wouldn't lie.

PUPHI. Where would Lakshmi know about these things.

MRS HATHIRAMANI. We don't know why. Why she would do it? – perhaps she has a friend who said too early to have a baby.

REKHA. No . . . No . . . It can't be.

SHAM. Auntie please just let it be. We'll talk to Lakshmi when she wakes up.

MRS HATHIRAMANI. But Sham, this business about her no longer being able to have children – we must keep that from her mother in law. I'm saying send her back to her in laws before they find out.

PUPHI. I was always against this match.

REKHA. They will find out sooner or later.

MRS HATHIRAMANI. Rekha if they divorce her think of Padma.

REKHA. She rang me – she was miscarrying – but how could I go to her when things are so difficult between us and the Samtanis.

SHAM. Mummy don't upset yourself.

MRS HATHIRAMANI. For what reason has she done this? It was only her first child and it would have made her place with them secure.

REKHA. She's so unhappy there. Poor child she doesn't understand – she can't come back. She's Hari's wife. What can I do?

MRS HATHIRAMANI. Behna Rekha budda – you send her back straight away, because you know if something goes wrong Mrs Bhagwandas and I can't be held responsible.

RAJU *enters with tiffin.*

RAJU. Memsahib.

MRS HATHIRAMANI. Raju, bring it here. We are all feeling hungry. Eat something Rekha. It's nice. See look at this. Sag bhaji and roti. Lovely home food.

MRS HATHIRAMANI. Come on Padma.

PADMA. No thanks Aunty.

MRS HATHIRAMANI. Dieting?

PADMA. No.

MRS HATHIRAMANI. Always these young girls are dieting nowadays. Eating only raw food and vegetables. Rekha, have something. Sham, you eat little daal and roti – it'll give you strength. Puphi thoro kha. It's very tasty. At least this much that donkey Raju has learned to cook.

PUPHI. I don't want anything. Not feeling hungry.

SWEEPER. Memsahib – shall I do the room now?

SHAM. No just leave it for today.

SWEEPER. Aatcha so I'll go.

MRS HATHIRAMANI. Raju – you go back home now and do your work. (*He exits.*) The whole time all he wants is education – always he is eating my head – Memsahib send me to school. I said nothing doing – why should I send him to school? – you tell me. Soon he will leave – servants never last.

REKHA. Sham – did you speak with the doctor? – did they tell you when she will wake up?

SHAM. Mama, they promised they'd phone.

MRS HATHIRAMANI. You can never trust these doctors nowadays. All they want is money.

SHAM. Mama you don't worry about the matter of the bill.

MRS HATHIRAMANI. Well it's going to come. The bill is going to come. I don't know who's going to pay.

*Ring at the door.* MRS SAMTANI *arrives.* PADMA *answers the door.*

PADMA. Namasté Auntie. Mama, Mrs Samtani's here.

REKHA. Namasté Mrs Samtani.

MRS SAMTANI. I don't understand, I get a phone call in Mahim – I had to get a taxi.

REKHA. Mr Hathiramani tried to ring you earlier – nobody was available. Lakshmi had to have an emergency.

MRS SAMTANI. What sort of emergency?

REKHA. She was haemorrhaging.

MRS SAMTANI. Aiee Ram! Is it the baby?

MRS HATHIRAMANI. Yes she lost the baby.

MRS SAMTANI. Aiee Allah!

SHAM. Couldn't you see that Lakshmi was ill? Why didn't you call us?

MRS SAMTANI. We didn't want to worry you unnecessarily.

PUPHI. But you knew she was ill.

MR SAMTANI. Well a week ago she had some bleeding and we called the doctor – there was no problem – she just had to rest.

PUPHI. Poor child – got no rest – worn out every time she came home.

REKHA. Puphi.

PUPHI. Sacho aaya. She treats her worse than a servant. The match was a mistake!

MR SAMTANI. For us it was a mistake! For you it was the best thing that happened!

MRS HATHIRAMANI. She is a good girl.

MR SAMTANI. She is nothing. Had we known the family circumstances we wouldn't have gone ahead with the match.

SHAM. You knew the deal and we fulfilled our part of it. Now you're making my sister's life hell.

MR SAMTANI. She has a very comfortable life considering you haven't settled for her.

MRS HATHIRAMANI. You saw the girl – the decision was yours.

MR SAMTANI. You tricked us.

MRS HATHIRAMANI. Our job was only to give a suggestion – we cannot be blamed for what has occurred.

PUPHI. You are the liars – you boasted about your wealth – you've got nothing. We were honest about what we could give.

MR SAMTANI. That is why only the first instalment has arrived and still we are waiting for the rest.

REKHA. This is not the time to argue about money. I have said before when Sham has more he will give.

SHAM. No Mama – we're not giving any more and Lakshmi will stay here – she's not going back to these people.

MR SAMTANI. Fine. You keep her. You can't settle for her – we don't want her. (*She leaves.*)

REKHA. Mrs Samtani. Mrs Samtani . . .

MRS HATHIRAMANI. Look Sham – you shouldn't be so hot-headed – you make it up with the Samtani's. Still they will take her back. They don't know she's had an abortion and can't have children.

SHAM. Mrs Hathiramani, with all due respect, I think this is a matter for our family.

MRS HATHIRAMANI. I'm only trying to help. Anyway you think about it. I'll send Raju for the tiffin later.

MRS HATHIRAMANI *exits.*

## Scene Twenty-One

*We follow* MRS HATHIRAMANI *back to her flat. It is now early evening. Heavy clouds, wind, thunder, lightning break through the scene.* MRS HATHIRAMANI *enters* – RAJU *is cleaning the chutney jars.*

MRS HATHIRAMANI. Gaddah! Are you from Tando Adam? That cloth is full of ants – you're putting back all the ants that you've just wiped out.

RAJU. It's very difficult Memsahib – why are you collecting all these old jars for me to clean? – There are so many ants.

MRS HATHIRAMANI. Don't be cheeky. It is the heat – they come out in the heat. Now you just do it properly. Go and wash the cloth. And later go upstairs and collect the tiffin. (*Entering bedroom.*) Hedan, they are blaming me for everything. I cooked them the food – arranged for their daughter when no one would have her and now things are going wrong. The mother in law is blaming me.

MR HATHIRAMANI. Thori shanti de. Let me finish this chapter. Just a bit of peace and quiet.

MRS HATHIRAMANI. I don't know what's going to happen. You know you are going spoil your eyes like that.

MR HATHIRAMANI. You will realise the importance of this one day.

MRS HATHIRAMANI. It is Saturn that is doing all this. Bhai Sahib says that before it moves out of The House Of The Sun, Shani will show its full strength.

MR HATHIRAMANI. One day it is Mrs Watumal – now you are back to Saturn – is there no end to your superstitious nonsense?

MRS HATHIRAMANI. I know you think I talk too much. But look what is happening – now you are becoming sick – Rahoo, dragon's head and Ketu dragon's tail are fighting over you, you don't eat, you don't sleep, you don't get up for your bath. We don't even know who is coming and going in Sadhbela because you have stopped taking notice.

MR HATHIRAMANI. These things are transitory – What are comings and goings to the immortal work of Shah Abdul Latif? 'Remove from our eyes the veil of ignorance and show us things as they really are'.

MRS HATHIRAMANI. Everything I have done properly. Pooja, fasting and seven thirty every morning I am down there with daal and sweetmeats for the cow.

MR HATHIRAMANI. I regret that I've never been able to influence you in one single way all these years we have spent together. I tried to get you to broaden your mind – go for education – keep up with your husband,.

MRS HATHIRAMANI. You Hyderbadi's have very liberal ideas – we were brought up to know our position with our husbands.

MR HATHIRAMANI. Should have had children – that would have kept you occupied.

MRS HATHIRAMANI. Yes I know you tried to throw me out because I can't have children.

MR HATHIRAMANI. You're still here aren't you?

MRS HATHIRAMANI. Haven't I looked after your house?

MR HATHIRAMANI. Han theek aie.

MRS HATHIRAMANI. Haven't I looked after you?

MR HATHIRAMANI. Han. Theek aie na. Theek aie.

MRS HATHIRAMANI. And I'm still looking after you. I am wearing this sapphire to protect us. Only a matter of three more weeks.

MR HATHIRAMANI. The more superstitious you get – the worse you are doing for yourself.

MRS HATHIRAMANI. I'm not doing anything. I don't even go out – have you seen me going to Crawford Market? I didn't even go to the hospital to see Lakshmi. Na, I don't go out. I just stay inside Sadhbela, then I'm protected from all this bad influence of Saturn. If I was in Sind, I would have gone to Sadhbela Island to the shrine and stayed there

MR HATHIRAMANI. Rest your brain – relax.

MRS HATHIRAMANI. I don't tax my brain – it is you. I only hope it doesn't burst open with everything filled inside.

MR HATHIRAMANI. Please Putali – now you just leave me.
I'm only on Song of The Necklace. Still there is Song of The
Lake, Song of The Desert, Song of Songs and the whole of
Latif's Risalo ahead of me. Whatever knowledge I have got,
I have to impart to our Sindhi brethren.

*There is a clap of thunder. She goes back to the kitchen.*

MRS HATHIRAMANI (*to* RAJU). Soon now we will have the
monsoon, maybe the rain will cool Sahib's mind. Bring me
the incense, Raju. You know today is purnima.

RAJU. What is that Memsahib?

MRS HATHIRAMANI. Full Moon. We have to do Satya
Naryan pooja.

RAJU. Why Memsahib?

MRS HATHIRAMANI. You don't ask why. It is the prayer.

RAJU. If I had education Memsahib – I would learn such things.
Please give me education.

MRS HATHIRAMANI. Look at your Sahib. See what education
is doing to him. Be glad you are free of it.

MRS HATHIRAMANI *lights the incense.*

MRS HATHIRAMANI. Bring me a thali, a little sindhoor and
some rice.

MR HATHIRAMANI. 'Latif the Sufi poet expresses himself in
the passionate language of a devoted lover – physical love
has to be raised to divine love.'

MRS HATHIRAMANI. Now Raju – you are making more
money than normally, because I don't go to Crawford Market
and you have to do the shopping – so you pocket the change
don't you? I know the prices.

RAJU. They charge me more.

MRS HATHIRAMANI. You don't have any brains? – You can't
talk? – You can't tell them to bring the price down?

*Clap of thunder.*

MR HATHIRAMANI. I am trying to work.

MRS HATHIRAMANI. Raju go and shut that window.

MR HATHIRAMANI. 'The mystic is a restless being – he is not satisfied with himself. He urges to be a pilgrim or a wanderer in search of a lost home'.

RAJU. Memsahib what is Sahib saying?

MRS HATHIRAMANI. It's his education talking. See all he does is write, write, write.

MRS HATHIRAMANI. Now I can light the diya and we can start. Put the rose petals there. Break the mithai, the Gods are hungry, we must feed them.

RAJU. Memsahib the ants will eat it.

MRS HATHIRAMANI. You just do what you're told – don't you want to learn?

MR HATHIRAMANI. 'The soul longs to find its perfect mate – the mystic craves perfection of heart otherwise is plunged in despondency'.

*There is a clap of thunder and a loud crash is heard from* MR HATHIRAMANI*'s room.*

MRS HATHIRAMANI. Hedan, are you all right? Raju go and see if your Sahib needs anything.

*He does so.*

RAJU. Memsahib, Sahib has burst his brains.

MRS HATHIRAMANI. Gaddah! don't try to be funny.

RAJU. Memsahib, come quickly. Sahib is dead.

MRS HATHIRAMANI (*going in*). Aiee Allah! Mr Hathiramani, are you all right? Don't just stand there, go and call Doctor Subramaniam – he never listens to me. It's all the Saturn – what more must we endure?

RAJU. Memsahib, he's not dead is he?

MRS HATHIRAMANI. Mua satch vachanch aao. Quickly go and get Dr. Sahib. Don't worry Ghansho, I am here. Everything will be all right.

## Scene Twenty-Two

*Three days have passed – it's Sunday 25th May.* PUMNANI*s flat.* REKHA *and* LAKSHMI *are there. Late afternoon.* RANI *rings the doorbell.*

RANI. Namasté Aunty.

REKHA. Hello Rani. Please come in.

RANI. I've just brought a few things.

REKHA. Oh how kind. Please come in. How are you?

RANI. Fine thank you. How's Lakshmi?

REKHA. She's OK. Come. She's going to be very pleased to see you. Lakshmi, Rani has come to see you.

RANI. Hi, how are you?

LAKSHMI. I'm all right. How have you suddenly remembered me?

RANI. Not suddenly. I'm in touch you know. I often bump into Sham and I always ask after you. Is he still at work?

LAKSHMI. Yes.

RANI. So what's it like being married?

LAKSHMI. OK. I must go soon Ama. I have to get back to cook the khana.

REKHA. Wait till Sham comes back. He'll take you. You can't go on the buses and trains on your own.

LAKSHMI. I can't wait for Sham Ama – they're expecting me.

RANI. Why don't you go by taxi?

REKHA. It's a very long way, we can't afford a taxi.

RANI. Oh. I'll take you. I don't mind. I'm not doing anything. I'll take her.

REKHA. That's very kind of you beta. God bless. I'll get her things.

RANI. What's happened? – I heard that you were in hospital – is everything all right?

LAKSHMI. I lost my baby.

RANI. Oh I'm sorry. Hari must be so upset. I hope he's looking after you.

LAKSHMI. You don't know do you?

RANI. What?

LAKSHMI. 1 can't have any more children.

RANI. Why, it was only a miscarriage.

LAKSHMI. Rani, if I tell you something do you promise you won't tell anybody.

RANI. Of course Lakshmi – I can keep a secret.

LAKSHMI. My mother in law didn't want me to have children – she wants Hari to divorce me because the dowry hasn't been settled. With the baby it would have been more difficult.

RANI. What are you saying Lakshmi?

LAKSHMI. My mother in law called a doctor to the house. I didn't know what was happening – she forced me to have an abortion.

RANI. You can't be serious!

LAKSHMI. She did.

RANI. But you can't go back Lakshmi!

LAKSHMI. But I have to go back. Ama has Puphi and Papa to look after and if I come home Padma will never get married.

RANI. Lakshmi, you've got to tell Aunty – She won't send you back if she knows.

LAKSHMI. Rani, everyone knows I had an abortion but Mama won't talk about it – she even thinks I might have arranged it myself because she knew I was unhappy there. Better for her to think that. You won't tell will you? You promised me.

RANI. Why are you protecting your in laws? – you should just take your things and leave – I wouldn't stay there.

LAKSHMI. Where would I go?

REKHA. Lakshmi – I've got your things for you.

LAKSHMI. OK Ama. Let's go Rani.

REKHA. Thank you so much Rani. Now beta look after yourself and send my namasté to Mrs Samtani.

*They exit – lights fade out on* RANI *and* LAKSHMI.


**Scene Twenty-Three**

*The Samtanis. Same day. Lights up on* MRS SAMTANI. RANI *and* LAKSHMI *arrive at the flat.*

LAKSHMI. Namasté Ama.

RANI. Hello Mrs Samtani.

MRS SAMTANI. Rani. You're the Murjani's girl. I didn't know that you knew Devki.

RANI. Yes we've been friends all our lives.

LAKSHMI. Stay for a while.

RANI. I can't stay very long.

MR SAMTANI. Of course you'll stay. You must have something to drink.

RANI. I've got a taxi waiting outside.

MR SAMTANI. Taxi can wait. Devki go and get Rani a drink. How are your parents?

RANI. Fine thank you.

MR SAMTANI. Your mother and I both sit on the committee for Sangam you know.

RANI. Oh!

MR SAMTANI. She does so much charity work.

LAKSHMI *comes back with bottles of drink.*

MR SAMTANI. Darling put it in a glass with some ice – do it nicely and make some bhajia.

RANI. No really I won't have anything.

MR SAMTANI. Let her do it.

RANI. No aunty – she's not well – she should be resting.

LAKSHMI. I'm fine Rani.

LAKSHMI *goes into kitchen.*

MR SAMTANI. You'll have to excuse her. Her family don't entertain very much. She's not used to it.

RANI. They're a very poor family actually.

MR SAMTANI. They're not poor. They're clever. You know they haven't even settled for Devki. That Sham working in Foreign for three years he must have it all stashed away somewhere and now working for Akbar Ali – he must be raking it in. My brothers just gave and gave to my in laws all their lives.

RANI. I don't agree with dowry. It's so archaic the way the girl's side always has to give and give.

MR SAMTANI. It's part of our culture – it's for settling the girl's future. Your mother must be already collecting for you.

RANI. I'm not having it.

MR SAMTANI. Look your mother loves you. How is she going to show that – of course she'll give. When we do kanyadan we're giving the flesh, body, full girl so we must give something along with that.

RANI. But if you can't afford it – the demand should not be there.

MR SAMTANI. We're not forcing anyone – the whole thing was agreed and they've cheated us.

RANI. They're not like that. I've known the Pumnani's all my life.

MR SAMTANI. From the day she came here she's been a burden in this family.

RANI. You're not being very fair.

MR SAMTANI. The girl can't even have children – she's barren. Why should my Hari stay with such a girl?

RANI. I really must be going.

MR SAMTANI. No no – the pakoras will be ready soon.

RANI. No the taxi's waiting. I really must go. Say bye to Lakshmi for me. I'll call her.

*She goes.*

MR SAMTANI. (*going into kitchen*) You've already been forever with the pakoras and your friend has already left. She was in such a hurry – God knows what you've been telling her. She didn't want to stay in this house. I suppose you went home snivelling to your family with stories again.

LAKSHMI. No Ama I haven't said anything.

MR SAMTANI. That's why everyone is gossiping about me. I suppose you told your friend it was me who made you lose the baby. No it was bad, it was unhealthy. You can't have children.

LAKSHMI. Ama, please don't stand so close the oil is hot.

MRS SAMTANI. It's not hot enough – put it higher – you can't fry pakoras unless it's really hot. Go on now put them in.

LAKSHMI. Ama please stand back from me it's spitting.

MR SAMTANI. I have to stand close because you don't know what you're doing. Go on throw them in.

LAKSHMI. The flame is too high.

MRS SAMTANI. Tai Ame. Vijina! Throw them in.

*There is a burst of fire and* LAKSHMI *screams.* RANI *turns back to see the fire. Blackout.*


**Scene Twenty-Four**

*The Funeral. The* SAMTANI'S *Flat.* PUMNANI'S, RANI, HATHIRAMANI'S *and* MR BHAGWANDAS *arrive one by one.* HARI *is already there. The body is laid out.*

MANTRA. Om namahah shambhavaiache
     Mayo bhavaiache
     Shankerotache
     Mayaskeroiache

Namahah shivaiache
Shivtehvaiache
Om shanti om shanti shanti

PUPHI. Pani.

MRS SAMTANI *comes with it and tries to dab* LAKSHMI.

PUPHI. This job is for her family. Come on Padma, Meena.

PADMA, MEENA, REKHA *and* PUPHI *dab* LAKSHMI.

MR HATHIRAMANI. Hari.

*HARI goes forward and puts paste on* LAKSHMI'*s brow,
eyes and ears and mouth. All of them come round and put
flowers at her head and her feet.*

REKHA. Mahinji vichari garib chokri! – Kishin and I were so
happy. We chose each other not to see this happen to our
children – this is not the way of things – parents should go
before their children.

MR HATHIRAMANI. Hari put the food with the body to start
her off in her next life.

*He does so.*

REKHA. Not even a pure funeral – prodded by doctors before
she could rest.

MRS HATHIRAMANI. She was a tikhur child – a daughter
born after three sons is very unlucky.

MRS HATHIRAMANI (*to* MRS SAMTANI). Something of
gold is also needed.

MRS SAMTANI. We are poor people – what gold can we give?

MEENA (*taking a charm from her necklace*). Here – take this.

PUPHI. Such a good girl – even died in the time of Shrad when
we are already in mourning for our departed souls.

REKHA. I kept sending her back – she'd say 'Mama, keep me
here, keep me here'. Every time I'd send her back.

MR HATHIRAMANI. Rekha behna – don't blame yourself – a
daughter comes into the family only as a guest to leave with
her doli when she enters her husband's house.

MRS HATHIRAMANI. Behna Hounsla rakh – she died a suhagan and not as a widow.

PUPHI. Put the wedding sari.

MRS SAMTANI *brings it and* PUPHI *takes it off her and lays it on* LAKSHMI.

SHAM. I really appreciate you being here, Dada Hathiramani.

MR HATHIRAMANI. Well, no hospital is going to keep me from my Sindhi brethren. 'For to the one that is born, death is certain, and certain is birth for one that has died. Therefore, for what is unavoidable, thou shouldst not grieve.' At least Kishin Bhau has been spared lifting his own daughter on to the funeral pyre.

SHAM. Papa is suffering also. He knows everything.

MANTRA. Om dhio Shanti Antrikshgwang
Shanti prithvi Shanti Rapah
Shanti Roshdhaya Shanti Vanaspatya
Shanti VishvahDevah Shanti Bramah
Shanti sarvagwang Shanti Shanti Revah
Shanti Sama Shanti Raydhi
Shanti Shanti Shanti.

*A mantra is sung.* MR HATHIRAMANI *and* SHAM *step forward and pick up the body, chanting as they exit slowly with it. We see* MRS SAMTANI *restrain* HARI.

MR HATHIRAMANI. Ram Nam. (*Repeat simultaneously with* SHAM.)

SHAM. Satya hè. (*Repeat simultaneously with* MR HATHIRAMANI.)

*The women wail as they exit.*


**Scene Twenty-Five**

*The* WATUMALS. *9th June – a mourning period of ten days has passed.*

MRS WATUMAL. How are they now upstairs?

SWEEPER. Rekha Memsahib is very upset. They have some sort of bad kismet in that family.

MRS WATUMAL. If the brother had settled it would never have happened.

LATA. Mama, don't discuss these things.

SWEEPER. Today the mourning is over but I don't think Lakshmi's soul is getting acceptance. It is restless because the in laws didn't perform all the proper rites.

MRS WATUMAL. We also heard Hari didn't go with the body.

MR WATUMAL. Well he's young they must be looking around for a new wife for him.

SWEEPER. Poor Sham Sahib – He wanted to scatter the ashes in the Ganges but the sea at Mahim was the best he could do.

MRS WATUMAL. Vichari chokri suthi thi!

SWEEPER. She was very nice to me. Rekha Memsahib has given me all her old clothes so it doesn't remind her of Lakshmi. It'll help me out – I can give it to my son and his wife.

*Bell rings and it is* SHAM.

LATA. Sham.

SHAM. Have I come at the wrong time?

LATA. No not at all. Come in.

SHAM. Akbar's just told me that he might be interested in your factory so I thought I'd tell you straight away.

LATA. That's great but you didn't have to come so soon – I know you're still in mourning.

SHAM. That's OK. I'm fine – I prefer to keep busy.

LATA. Well if you're sure – Papa's here but Mohan's not back yet. Papa – good news – Akbar Ali might be interested in a partnership with us.

MR WATUMAL. Puther, sit down. Lata, get Sham a drink.

SUNITA. Hey listen to this – Joan Collins is getting married again. She's 58 and she's getting married.

82

MRS WATUMAL. Who to?

SUNITA. Oh some young toy boy. Mama, she's your age and she's just getting married.

MOHAN *enters.*

MOHAN. I don't believe this yaar. Last night you talk to me about the plans and now you're invading my house – you're a true dark horse yaar.

MRS WATUMAL. Lata – get something for your brother.

MOHAN. Get me an ashtray.

MR WATUMAL. Akbar Ali – I'm still worried about his reputation.

SHAM. Mr Watumal, you have no problem there.

MOHAN. There's a lot of mileage in what the boy's saying – I've studied the plans – lot of mileage.

MR WATUMAL. You've changed your tune!

MOHAN. I've had to rethink my strategy, Now we're in a totally different ball game. I was discussing it with Homi and Ranjit – the rest houses can wait till the factory generates some capital.

MR WATUMAL. It's good you're taking an interest now. Lata can stay at home.

SHAM. But uncle, she knows the factory inside out –

MOHAN. Lata can work in the factory but she doesn't have any business sense.

LATA. They're my plans.

SHAM. The details of the merger are Lata's work – she's indispensable to this project.

MRS WATUMAL. You should stay at home.

SUNITA. No mother – let her go to work – she wants to run the country next.

LATA. Papa – this is our last chance, we should meet with Akbar Ali.

MOHAN. I don't mind this joint venture but we'd have to have total control.

SHAM. Sure, the factory's still going to be run by you people. A.A. would only be interested in being a sleeping partner.

MR WATUMAL. I want to ask one thing. Why is someone like Akbar Ali interested in our business?

SHAM. Mr Watumal – he's done the same thing with Rebotco and soon it will show a profit.

MR WATUMAL. Profit – that's a word I had forgotten.

LATA. Papa, we've discussed this – we need an injection of cash otherwise we might as well do as Mohan says and declare hands up.

MR WATUMAL. OK theek ai – we'll meet him but let's see.

SHAM. I've made an appointment for 9 am tomorrow – we'll go that side and take it from there.

MRS WATUMAL. Lata – go with Sham – take the lentils and spinach for Rekha. Please tell her I have a migraine otherwise I would have come myself.

MOHAN. I'd prefer if he came this side. Meet him at the factory.

SHAM. Yah no problem.

LATA *returns.*

OK Aunty.

*They exit.*


## Scene Twenty-Six

RANI, PINKY *and* SUSHU *in* RANI's *bedroom. Same day –*
*7th June.*

PINKY. Does your mother always leave the door open like this?

RANI. Yeah, I can't do anything in here.

SUSHU. Shut it yaar – I want to have a cigarette.

PINKY. Let her peer. What can she see? So has the publicity died down yet?

RANI. Finally yes. I hate people staring and pointing at me.

SUSHU. Has anyone asked you for your autograph?

RANI. No not yet.

SUSHU. I'm sure Gopal will.

PINKY. You went to court yah?

RANI. Yaar I had to – I was the only witness.

SUSHU. What did they ask you?

RANI. You know, what I saw.

PINKY. It was the mother in law wasn't it?

RANI. I don't know.

SUSHU. But you saw it didn't you?

RANI. I did but I mean I couldn't tell what happened just before the fire. In any case the verdict was accidental death.

PINKY. You know I think we should do an exposé on this. Rani's seen it first hand.

RANI. I've had quite enough thank you very much.

PINKY. Too many dowry deaths occur at that socio-economic level. Somebody should write an article about it.

SUSHU. Why don't you write it then?

PINKY. I think I will.

RANI. No no – Lakshmi was my friend.

PINKY. Come on – she was murdered by her mother in law.

RANI. I don't want to talk about it – let's change the subject.

SUSHU. You see the problem is people don't want to talk about it so it keeps happening. So what did you wear on the day of the hearing then?

RANI. What does it matter?

SUSHU. I just want to know.

RANI. Well I couldn't wear my jeans – you know what my mother's like.

PINKY. Did she go with you?

RANI. Oh God yes.

PINKY. With her diamonds?

RANI. She did yeh – I told her not to – I said it was a bit tacky.

SUSHU. Did you keep any of the newspaper cuttings?

RANI. No but Mummy did. She promptly made a file.

PINKY. I bet she's jealous. You've got more publicity than she's ever had out of her charity dos.

RANI. Yeh I know.

PINKY. So what about Sham? – you took my advice and threw yourself at him?

RANI. Do you mind, I didn't.

PINKY. I told you to.

RANI. No no wait wait – do you want to hear the whole story – see it was like this. I took him down to Walkeshwar Tank – I got his attention – we'd just started getting a conversation going and suddenly he just grabs my neck and he starts kissing me. It was so embarrassing – I didn't know what to do.

SUSHU. Was it a Frenchie?

RANI. I wish. So funny though. I was so embarrassed. Anyway I said, look Sham I'm not really interested you know.

PINKY. Oh yes.

RANI. I'm not.

PINKY. I'm sure she's twisting the tale.

RANI. I'm not twisting anything. Anyway it gets better. My mother came running after me – can you imagine – Mum in her georgette sari running round the beach. It was so funny.

SUSHU. Did you get grounded?

RANI. Actually – she took it out on Sham.

PINKY. So what about Kamal? Heard you had a tea party?

RANI. Shut up.

PINKY. Come on. I know everything.

RANI. It was so ironic. I said to my mother – I don't want to talk about marriage and then she takes me to the Taj with Mrs Prem Chand and who should the prospective turn out to be – Kamal – I couldn't believe it.

PINKY. What a coincidence – we had such a laugh about it.

RANI. My mother was furious – firstly Kamal's related to you guys and secondly she says Kamal's mother dresses like a Parsi.

SUSHU. So you've fallen in love?

RANI. It's not that heavy, yah.

PINKY. Let's face it you're going to be a bored Sindhi housewife. Shopping in London, dieting in Lagos.

RANI. Yah terrible isn't it?

SUSHU. So when's it going to be official?

RANI. Quite soon. Well Papa's very keen – Kamal's parents have got two factories and they'll be able to do a tie up. Even Mom's come round – she's giving me a maid to take with me for my wedding present.

PINKY. Who would have thought – radical Rani having an A.M. with a nice Sindhi boy.

RANI. Well I don't want to end up on the shelf like the Watumal sisters. I'm going abroad – Kamal says I can study.

PINKY. You don't have to justify it Rani – most Sindhi girls have a rebellious phase and then end up doing what's expected of them.

SUSHU. Shut up Pinky – at least she's found someone nice. God knows who you'll end up with.

PINKY. I'll end up with whoever I want to end up with.

RANI. We're honeymooning in Paris. I'll send you dolls a postcard.

SUSHU. I'm so envious.

RANI. Well when I'm settled in The States you'll all have to come over and see me.


**Scene Twenty-Seven**

*The Hospital. Four days have passed. It's June 11th.*

MRS HATHIRAMANI. Aajo tavanji tabeyat ken aaye? I've brought your favourite cashew nut sweets.

MR HATHIRAMANI. How many times have I said I'm not allowed these things?

MRS HATHIRAMANI. Why?

MR HATHIRAMANI. Can't you read? – of course you can't – 'Special Diet'.

MRS HATHIRAMANI. Oh.

MR HATHIRAMANI. I can't eat this. It is very bad for me.

MRS HATHIRAMANI. They don't know what they are doing – I bring this food – good food for you – to give you strength – then I can take you home. Eat a little.

MR HATHIRAMANI. I can't eat it – you want to kill me?

MRS HATHIRAMANI. Why do you say these things to me? You think I'm trying to kill you? You think I'm not a good wife. You don't even let me stay here to look after you. A wife should be by her husband. What will people say?

MR HATHIRAMANI. That's Rohri village mentality – who cares what people will say? Now take this away from me – I can't eat it. It's my diabetes.

MRS HATHIRAMANI. Once Saturn moves out of The House of The Sun – you'll be well.

MR HATHIRAMANI. Saturn is going to go but he's going to take me with him.

MRS HATHIRAMANI. Tomorrow is the last day of Shani and Bhai Sahib says it is showing no leniency so I have to do all these things at home. I'll do all the purification before you come.

MR HATHIRAMANI. I need some rest.

MRS HATHIRAMANI. You have enough rest in the hospital.

MR HATHIRAMANI. Yes and peace of mind.

MRS HATHIRAMANI. How do you rest when so many people are coming here. Mr Watumal, P.B. Bhau – you let them come. I come like a visitor.

MR HATHIRAMANI. They are coming with very important co-operative business. Aatcha listen – I want you to go and see Mrs Watumal and take a proposal on behalf of the co-op.

MRS HATHIRAMANI. I'm not going to see that woman.

MR HATHIRAMANI. Just do one good deed in your life. Propose to them that the co-operative has decided that in the light of recent events we must look after the children of Sadhbela – propose Padma Pumnani for Mohan Watumal.

MRS HATHIRAMANI. That good for nothing loafer. What a stupid idea.

MR HATHIRAMANI. Why stupid?

MRS HATHIRAMANI. You yourself didn't want Mohan in your family and now you are recommending him to someone else.

MR HATHIRAMANI. We are reassured the boy is a changed character so he's now worthy of the effort we are putting. Besides he has expressed interest in Padma.

MRS HATHIRAMANI. What about Padma? She's a young girl and he's in his thirties.

MR HATHIRAMANI. With her sister dying in mysterious circumstances she can do no better than Mohan.

MRS HATHIRAMANI. What about dowry? – you know Mrs Watumal will be wanting dowry.

MR HATHIRAMANI. The members of the co-op will put up the dowry – we will negotiate on behalf of the girl – half sai in accordance with status of both families.

MRS HATHIRAMANI. That is not going to be enough – Mrs Watumal is collecting for her girls.

MR HATHIRAMANI. There is too much greed in these matters – look what happened to Lakshmi – it will suffice. You must also go and speak to Rekha and tell her it is not an act of charity. After all their children are our children.

MRS HATHIRAMANI. Mrs Watumal is our enemy and you are trying to help her. I am not going to do this. You and your co-op sort it.

**Scene Twenty-Eight**

*The next day. June 12th. Morning. On the terrace.*

SUNITA. Why are you looking at me like that?

LATA. Just wondering what's going on in your little head.

SUNITA. Why don't you just come out with it – you've heard.

LATA. Why are you doing it?

SUNITA. What do you mean?

LATA. You want to get married to this man who's so old.

SUNITA. Forty-five.

LATA. And he's got three kids.

SUNITA. Only one of them is still at home.

LATA. Sunita – why are you so desperate to get married?

SUNITA. I've been sitting here on my arse for the past ten years waiting that's why. According to Mrs Bhagwandas – he's forty-five, he's got a business going – just one child at home and I'm happy with that. So don't make judgements.

LATA. He just wants someone to look after the kids.

SUNITA. How do you know?

LATA. What would he want to marry you for?

SUNITA. I'm quite in demand at the moment. Lots of men are looking for second wives.

LATA. Exactly.

SUNITA. What's your problem – you want to be a spinster all
your life? Anyway I don't know what you are cribbing about.
I've seen the way you look at Sham. Cradle snatcher!

LATA. We meet because we have a mutual interest in the
business. Anyway he's too young.

SUNITA. So there is a little spark there?

LATA. Look Sunita, I used to be like you. I used to feel I
wanted to get married but I got fed up being bandied about
and then being rejected.

SUNITA. There's another one being found for you.

LATA. No way and I'm certainly not marrying a divorcee.

SUNITA. You better tell Mrs Bhagwandas that because she's
looking.

LATA. I'm not getting married.

SUNITA. Fine, fine – you be a dried up spinster all your life –
I'm getting married.


**Scene Twenty-Nine**

*Same day. June 12th.* RAJU *is coming up in the lift with tiffin
having just come from the hospital.*

GOPAL. How is your father?

RAJU. He's sent Memsahib's food back – he's got sweet blood
– diabetes.

GOPAL. I'm totally broke sala. Since your father burst his
brains my income's gone down – no money for chai paani,
can't afford foreign – have to smoke local.

RAJU *arrives at the* HATHIRAMANI'*s flat and goes in.*

RAJU. Memsahib what shall I do with this? Sahib sent it back.

MRS HATHIRAMANI. Throw it away. He never eats my food –
he wants boiled food from the hospital.

RAJU. I can eat it Memsahib. No need to waste it.

MRS HATHIRAMANI. You go and do what I have told you.

RAJU. Shall I make some tea?

MRS HATHIRAMANI. No I don't want tea.

RAJU. I'll get you Thumbs Up.

MRS HATHIRAMANI. I don't want anything. Leave me alone.

RAJU. Memsahib what's the matter?

MRS HATHIRAMANI. I have to do all this purification before your Sahib comes home. Bhai Sahib has gone to Nasik and I don't know what to do. Saturn is giving me too much tension on my brain.

RAJU. I'll help you do the pooja.

MRS HATHIRAMANI. No I have done all that and it is not calming me down. Still I have the depression, mui garmi – the rain also is refusing to come.

RAJU. When Sahib comes everything will be all right.

MRS HATHIRAMANI. Yes till the next time he gets overheated with too much work.

*Pause.*

Raju – when Sahib's brain burst open – what was he doing?

RAJU. Memsahib, he was writing in his diary.

MRS HATHIRAMANI. Yes, he was sitting here and writing in his diary. The whole day he was writing in his diary. Bring me some coal and a bucket. The big one ayah uses to wash the clothes. And light the coals. Bring it quickly. He doesn't care for me. He cares for his diaries.

*She's destroying the diaries.* RAJU *returns. She sets the diaries alight.*

Chordo! Leave it. Now fan it. Fan it a little. Pankha diyo! I'm going to destroy this bloody diary – diary, diary, diary, – the whole day is diary.

RAJU. Sahib will be very angry.

MRS HATHIRAMANI. Nobody else but diary. Fan it! Fan it! Pankha diyo! We have to destroy this.

RAJU. I'm frightened.

MRS HATHIRAMANI. You are frightened to do God's work. Do as I tell you. We have to burn it all before Mr Hathiramani comes home.

RAJU. Memsahib – it's dangerous.

MRS HATHIRAMANI. Then take it out on the balcony. Fan it! Fan it!

RAJU. Memsahib! Memsahib! Look Memsahib! Dekho! Dekho! Now we have done it!

MRS HATHIRAMANI. Abhi humara luck change hoyega. All the good luck will come to us – All the good luck.

*Mr and* MRS WATUMAL *arrive from downstairs having noticed something burning.*

MRS WATUMAL. Oh Mrs Hathiramani are you trying to kill us?

MRS HATHIRAMANI. What the hell are you doing here. Get out!

MR WATUMAL. Raju, get water. Pani!

MRS WATUMAL. You're trying to set the whole building on fire!

MRS HATHIRAMANI. I'm not setting fire to your house. It's my home. I can burn it down if I please – what's it to you?

MR WATUMAL. Raju, water.

RAJU. Sahib, coming.

MRS WATUMAL. I always knew you are trying to kill us. You've ruined my son's life.

MRS HATHIRAMANI. Your idle son loafs about. Like father like son.

MRS WATUMAL. And your man – he's burst his brains!

MRS HATHIRAMANI. How do you know?

MRS WATUMAL. Aré, the whole building knows.

MRS HATHIRAMANI. Say what you like, your boy is unmarriageable and so are the girls.

MRS WATUMAL. You're just jealous – you haven't got any children – that's why you're trying to burn us down.

MRS HATHIRAMANI. Why would I want to burn you down? This is all because of Saturn. For this reason there is fire, not to destroy your house.

MRS WATUMAL. What about my son? You've ruined his marriage prospects.

MRS HATHIRAMANI. We only told the truth – you took it badly. Now Saturn is leaving The House Of The Sun even your Mohan will be settled.

MRS WATUMAL. Now what are you up to?

MRS HATHIRAMANI. You know Mr Hathiramani is the secretary of the co-op. He has decided to fix up someone for Mohan.

MRS WATUMAL. You don't interfere.

MRS HATHIRAMANI. OK fine – he's your son – keep him, nobody else wants him.

MRS WATUMAL. Who is the girl?

MRS HATHIRAMANI. Sit down. É Raju Gaddah! Can't you hear – bring a Thumbs Up, a cold one. Padma – good family, just bad luck since they came here.

MRS WATUMAL. Padma – but they've no money.

MRS HATHIRAMANI. What respect the Pumnani's had in Sind.

MRS WATUMAL. That was in Sind.

MRS HATHIRAMANI. Who knew you in Sind?

MRS WATUMAL. Where's the dowry coming from?

MRS HATHIRAMANI. The brothers from the co-op. Don't worry nobody's asking from you. Money is about to enter your house.

RAJU *comes with drinks.*

MRS HATHIRAMANI. I'll talk to Rekha today.

MRS WATUMAL. I'll come with you.

MRS HATHIRAMANI. There's no need. Let me talk to her first. You know that me and Jashoti Behn look after our children. There's a good boy and there's a good girl – we think of that.

MR WATUMAL. It looked worse than it was – only the curtains and books have gone. Everything else is saved.

MRS HATHIRAMANI. Are many books left?

MR WATUMAL. Unfortunately not. Hathiramani Bhau will feel this badly.

RAJU. Memsahib it is raining. Now the monsoon has begun.

MRS HATHIRAMANI. Han. Om.

*Sound of heavy rain – lights fade to black.*


**Scene Thirty**

*Two days later. June 14th. It is still raining. The* HATHIRA-MANI'S *flat.*

RAJU. Memsahib, how many chapatis am I making?

MRS HATHIRAMANI. Well.

MR HATHIRAMANI (*calling*). Raju É Raju.

RAJU. Sahib.

MR HATHIRAMANI. Where is my diary?

MRS HATHIRAMANI. It must have burned in the fire probably. Everything is burned. But nothing can harm you now. Saturn is gone. Sahib only has to eat English food. Boiled. Everything boiled. Beans boiled and carrots boiled.

RAJU. Memsahib, how many chapatis do I make?

MRS HATHIRAMANI. Well how many are you going to eat?

RAJU. You know I only eat two.

MRS HATHIRAMANI. Well I had tea and samosas so I'm not very hungry – all right make three for me and one dry chapati for Sahib. Raju, you know I made a suka to Saint Jhulelal –

when Saturn left the House of the Sun I vowed to do something good.

RAJU. You'll give me money to hire a bicycle?

MRS HATHIRAMANI. Gaddah listen. I'm going to send you to night school for education.

RAJU. I don't want education – I've changed my mind.

MRS HATHIRAMANI. You are exactly like gaddah – donkey – exactly. When you wanted education and I said no, you wanted it. Now I'm saying go for education, you don't want it.

RAJU. I'll stay here and cook chapatis.

MRS HATHIRAMANI. You'll still cook chapatis – you're only going to night school.

RAJU. No Memsahib, I don't want my brains to burst.

MRS HATHIRAMANI. You shut up and do that. (*She crosses the bedroom.*) Heddan – you've only just come back from the hospital – you need to rest.

MR HATHIRAMANI. How can I rest? I am a Sindhi. We have lost everything, even lost our homeland when we were forced to flee. We Sindhis always have to adapt.

MRS HATHIRAMANI. Han.

MR HATHIRAMANI. While we have overcome adverse circumstances, our culture is becoming a melting pot. Our people think they are very cosmopolitan, they marry Chinese, speak English and eat Japanese food, but they don't know where they come from. Our Sindhi civilisation is the most ancient in the world. Do the young people know about our great Sindhi city Mohenjodaro which stood on the banks of the Indus three hundred years before Christ? Do they know it was a Sindhi who wounded Alexander the Great and forced his retreat from our land? The very first man, even in the English Dictionary it is written, was in Sind. We Sindhis can adapt to any circumstances. There isn't a country in the world where you won't find a Sindhi merchant or trader.

MRS HATHIRAMANI. What are the Sindhis in Foreign to you?

MR HATHIRAMANI. Don't you see? We must keep the Sind in our hearts. I have to reach the expat Sindhis all over the world, in London, New York, Hong Kong, Lagos, Madrid. Our Sinduvarkis have been trading abroad for centuries but there is no unification. É Raju – bring a box. Bring a big box and put all these things away – I'm going to have a printing press here.

MRS HATHIRAMANI. What?

MR HATHIRAMANI. Printing press.

MRS HATHIRAMANI. Where are you going to put it? As it is we haven't got enough room.

MR HATHIRAMANI. From tomorrow I'm working on a newsletter for all Sindhis – 'The Ubiquitous Sindhi'.

MRS HATHIRAMANI. I thought all your diary business was over.

MR HATHIRAMANI. Forget the diary. Through my newsletter expat Hindu Sindhis will rise and consolidate.

MRS HATHIRAMANI. Calm down or again your health will suffer.

MR HATHIRAMANI. From tomorrow you sleep in the other room, all right?

MRS HATHIRAMANI. What?

MR HATHIRAMANI. I need peace and quiet to work.

MRS HATHIRAMANI. You wouldn't let me sleep near you in the hospital and now in my own home!

MR HATHIRAMANI. Off you go.

MRS HATHIRAMANI. For food shall I call you?

MR HATHIRAMANI. Call me.

MRS HATHIRAMANI. Raju, finish stringing those beans. Bhai Sahib is back from Nasik. I need to see him.

*She exits and climbs down the stairs to* BHAI SAHIB*'s as the lights fade to blackout, and she calls:*

MRS HATHIRAMANI. Bhai Sahib – O Bhai Sahib.

*Finis.*